TALKING ABOUT ORACY

Developing communication beyond the classroom

SARAH DAVIES

First Published 2020

by John Catt Educational Ltd,
15 Riduna Park, Station Road,
Melton, Woodbridge IP12 1QT

Tel: +44 (0) 1394 389850
Email: enquiries@johncatt.com
Website: www.johncatt.com

Opinions expressed in this publication are those
of the contributors and are not necessarily those
of the publishers or the editors. We cannot accept
responsibility for any errors or omissions.

ISBN: 978 1 913622 37 4

Set and designed by John Catt Educational Limited

TESTIMONIALS

As someone who is passionate about everyone finding their voice, I found this book refreshing and one that every educator across the globe should read. In my opinion, oracy can be all too easily forgotten – the poor relation to numeracy and literacy – yet it is a vital life skill that our young people have to be taught. As Sarah says, 'it is time that we talk about oracy', and her book does this wonderfully well. With case studies, research and clear explanations, *Talking About Oracy* is an enjoyable and engaging read. With her top tips and wise words, Sarah has ensured that this book will improve our students' capacity to understand speech and to express themselves in speech, but she has also considered how we (as educators) can improve our own skills too. With a chapter devoted to oracy in leadership, this book meets the needs of all those in education and I cannot recommend it enough. I just wish it had been out when I first started teaching!

Toria Bono, primary teacher and evidence lead educator

Talking About Oracy is a much-needed book, especially for secondary school teachers and leaders. As a former English and drama teacher, many of my own light-bulb moments with students were when I saw what they were able to achieve when supported to talk and communicate effectively. Sarah makes an effective case for all teachers to teach oracy both as a crucial life skill and as a process of learning. The book and the case studies it contains are rooted in research and evidence whilst offering resources to apply such knowledge practically. It's definitely a book for your CPD library.

Vivienne Porritt, leadership consultant, strategic leader of #WomenEd, vice president of Chartered College of Teaching, @ViviennePorritt

This fascinating book takes a research-informed approach to the issues of developing a culture of oracy in our schools. Sarah carefully and skilfully demonstrates the need for oracy to be in the forefront of our minds before explaining how it might be approached in a range of contexts and to meet different needs.

This book acknowledges the debates that occur around different approaches to teaching and different opinions on the purpose of education whilst showing that whatever your stance, oracy has a place at the heart of our classroom and school practice.

Every teacher will find something useful to take away, mull over, and implement in their classroom.

Mark Enser, head of geography and research lead at Heathfield Community College, author of *Generative Learning in Action*.

Oracy is such an important topic at the moment, with lots of us relying on conversation more than ever. The rewards from a strong culture of oracy are innumerable. Vygotsky suggests that talk represents our thoughts; therefore, the higher the quality of our students' speech, the higher the quality of their thinking. What Sarah Davies does here is unpick the complicated and nuanced world of communication. She expresses with clarity and confidence the strategic vision to support oracy within your provision and does so with humour, honesty and intelligence. This is a must buy for any teacher or leader looking to improve outcomes for all students.

Laura Markendale, deputy head teacher at a multi-academy trust

CONTENTS

ACKNOWLEDGEMENTS

Throughout my career, I've been fortunate to have gained so much through quite literally standing on the shoulders of giants. From the leadership teams that have encouraged me to progress to the colleagues who have supported me, I am fortunate and thankful for the professional career I've already had, whilst still being excited for what's to come!

Working with exemplary practitioners like Maria and Rachel has given me the courage to venture into writing this book. With friends like Robert, Sophie and Zoya, I've learned so much about teaching and they've been with me on this journey right from the start. I also need to provide a special mention for Charlie. Her patience, support, way with words and ability to read extensive amounts of my work whilst keeping me focussed have made this book possible!

Finally, none of this would be possible without the support and encouragement of my family. To my mother who shaped me, I'll be forever thankful. To my husband who is the calmest, most rational person I have ever met – your ability to put up with me still is extraordinary! To my boys – little will you know that none of this would have been possible without you both. Being a mother to you has made me the person I am today. You both make me a better person and I hope that you always remember that your mummy loves you to infinity and beyond.

PREFACE

When I consider the reason why I chose to focus my book specifically on the necessity of oracy skills in the classroom, I'm inclined to think back to an experience I had when I first started out on my path to teaching. Working closely with a student for whom English was an additional language, my role as a teaching assistant was fairly simple; I had to ensure that this student would be able to access mainstream education and consequently the GCSE examinations.

As we began to work through the objectives and the more structured responses, I noticed that the student was beginning to withdraw from their studies. It was explained to me that because this student wasn't proficient in the English language, they had been led to believe that this would mean they would be unable to aim for higher aspirational goals. The student firmly believed that their life choices would be hindered by their ability to communicate. This perception caused me to quickly banish the idea that our time together should focus on being 'exam ready'. Instead, we began to work on interview preparation, tone, dialogue and body language. As the student's confidence soared, so, ironically enough, did their academic ability. A student who had initially explained that they would work in the family's shop and local gym went on to university to study engineering.

I'm not taking responsibility for this student's immense achievements. This has always simply been a reminder to me that in order to take a step forward you sometimes just have to take a step back. There was no point in developing subject knowledge until the fundamental principles of learning and communication were established. Consequently, this is now an ethos I follow with all my students.

What was ironic about this experience was that, as I was supporting this particular student, I too was being exposed to potential aspirational goals that I could achieve if I only aimed higher. By being asked my opinion, included in professional discussions, and encouraged to enrol on a teaching course, I too was being given a voice.

I remind myself of this whenever I contemplate why I chose this profession. I think it's important for all of us to remind ourselves that education isn't the end goal, but a brief section of a much longer journey. What is so significant about this quest is the variety of paths that we can expose our students to, and how we have the ability to provide them with the confidence to venture in any direction that they choose.

It is through oracy skills that we can show our students that one of the fundamental skills to succeed in life is the ability to communicate in whatever form is necessary. No person should ever see themselves as an island. It is through communication that we can therefore encourage not only the progression of others, but also our own development, whether this be as a practitioner, a mentor or a leader.

TALKING ABOUT ORACY – AN INTRODUCTION

Oracy in British English

(ˈɔːrəsɪ)

NOUN

The capacity to express oneself in and understand speech

Collins English Dictionary. Copyright © HarperCollins Publishers

Word origin

C20: from Latin *or-*, *os* mouth, by analogy with *literacy*

It is time for us to talk about oracy.

When we think about the transferable skills all students should take with them when they leave education, oracy, literacy and numeracy should logically stand proudly side by side. This triad of skill sets contains the key components used to measure intellectual development in childhood, and is further nurtured in all students throughout their education. However, when we consider that the recognition of these three separate skill sets has (at the time of writing) only been in existence for the past 55 years, we begin to recognise that oracy is still very much in its infancy in regard to its being viewed as an explicit staple in all academic establishments.

Coined by Andrew Wilkinson in 1965 at Birmingham University, the term oracy came into being in response to the lack of importance being placed on speaking and listening skills in education. With the focus on reading and writing, the failure to represent spoken language development meant a crucial life skill was being neglected. Thus a separate recognition evolved that considered the significance of communication in more detail.

Oracy can be recognised as both an outcome and a process of learning, which is why its implementation is crucial to development. With younger children, oracy can typically be seen predominantly as an outcome. A child's ability in spoken language and communication can be used to gauge their level of development. Once the basic ability of communication has then been acquired, the significance of oracy shifts more towards its recognition as a process of learning.

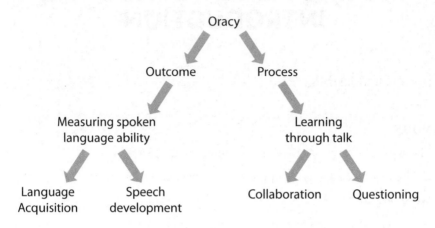

For too long, the focus of the curriculum has been on the stress and rigour of assessments and the fulfilment of the curriculum to ensure that all students can access their GCSE examinations. This book will consider the various components of what can be considered the implementation of effective oracy skills. It will:

- question whether an approach to learning that fails to take oracy into account could have a detrimental effect on students who may have been exposed to fewer of the skills that they will require when leaving an educational setting and venturing into everyday life.

- address behavioural concerns that teachers may have regarding dialogic teaching strategies and support leaders with embracing mastery of oracy across the curriculum to develop students' life skills.

- consider how we can model oracy skills and use them to explore leadership strategies and approaches to professional dialogue.

In recent years, there appears to have emerged a distinct difference between those schools that have chosen to encourage the implementation of oracy strategies into their curriculum and those that have chosen to focus more specifically on skills conducive to written assessments. By shining a light on the effective practices that are being adopted in these settings, it is hoped that we can begin to acknowledge the vital role of communication and how both we and our students can communicate effectively.

In 2020, oracy appears to have even less relevance in academia. As a result of a nationwide lockdown due to a pandemic, the education system in the United Kingdom has been left wading through the dark and uncharted waters of substantial missed learning time. In response to this, it was decided that the cohort would not be expected to provide any recorded proof of the spoken language component. What was previously a crucial element of the historic English Language GCSE had already become the hindrance of a subject-specific curriculum. What should have been a skill set that is encouraged and embedded in all subjects was cast to the realms of an inconvenient 'add-on'. The only support offered to alleviate the pressure of the GCSEs for the 2020/2021 cohort was to remove the need for visual evidence of spoken language tasks to be provided.

Schools that perceive oracy as an 'add-on' need to be exposed to the realistic interpretation of how oracy can and has been implemented in academic settings across the country. With the incorporation of these strategies, the hope is that we can embrace the idea that this skill is a necessity for the success of all learners both during and after their education. Training students in the ability to communicate effectively with different audiences in different contexts needs to be brought back into the spotlight.

By explicitly teaching and engaging with oracy skills, we can therefore help our students in much more that their summative educational assessments. By adopting these strategies, we will consequently support them in:

- developing their confidence in communicating with a variety of audiences.
- contributing to a positive and proactive attitude to learning.
- a reduction in anxiety through our encouragement of positive discussions that focus on the sharing of thoughts and feelings.
- expressing their thoughts and feelings in a more structured and approachable manner.
- building an understanding of social issues and being able to share ideas and perspectives.
- providing strategies that can be used to encourage restorative discussions or to manage difficult conversations effectively.

- collaborating with others and maintaining a dialogue with peers that can develop into friendship as well as encouraging future professional networking.
- the ability to recognise spoken language techniques including debating skills and the incorporation of rhetoric language to match purpose.
- the ability to develop critical thinking through communication and dialogue that encourages further development.
- expanding employment opportunities through the ability to communicate in professional settings.

The Education Endowment Foundation (EEF) suggested that, alongside supporting these capabilities, the incorporation of oracy education can actually improve student results. In particular, the effect on pupil premium students was substantial, given the encouragement that oracy can provide in the development of one's ability to explore and question learning for a more critical understanding (Jay et al., 2017).

But why?

The recognition and incorporation of oracy into the curriculum in all stages of education doesn't just lead to a positive impact on the students. The more we embrace and master these skills, the more we begin to establish how we as practitioners can also benefit from their implementation:

- The ability to provide verbal feedback can result in a reduction in workload.
- The ability to model effective oracy skills will help to support both colleague and student conversations, promoting focussed and meaningful dialogue.
- Embracing oracy skills can also promote established behaviour management strategies and opportunities for restorative dialogues.
- Recognising and encouraging oracy skills can also support staff/ colleague health and wellbeing as well as the health and wellbeing of surrounding colleagues.

The relationship between oracy and improvement of outcomes (not just academically focussed) can also be identified by the building of the teacher-student relationship. In 2016, Pearson research into the qualities of an effective teacher concluded that relationships were key to forming strong and reciprocal foundations on which learning can take place. It is the ability to develop a connection with the learner that equips teachers with the confidence to progress and develop.

Important qualities of an effective teacher	Parents	Students	Teachers
Relationships	19.2%	25.2%	17.8%
Patient, caring	15.3%	9.9%	7.9%
Engaging	7.6%	9.4%	7.5%
Subject knowledge	9.4%	6.0%	7.0%
Knowledge of learners	7.1%	9.3%	7.2%
Professionalism	4.6%	4.5%	8.0%
Class management	4.2%	3.9%	7.1%
Make ideas clear	6.1%	5.2%	5.3%
Dedication	5.1%	5.7%	4.9%

(Pearson 2016, p. 17)

Out of all of the contributing factors that were considered throughout the research, the three dominant elements were:

- the ability to develop relationships
- the perception of being kind and caring
- the ability to engage with learners.

Consequently, based on the necessity for communication skills to encourage relationships, it is the embodiment of spoken language into our pedagogical approaches and the recognition of its significance that enables us to become effective practitioners.

Oracy is not, and should never be, perceived as a subject-specific skill. It is not an assessment-based unit that fits neatly into the curriculum, but an overarching process that can help to support and develop our students, our leadership capabilities, and our ability to communicate with others.

Throughout early development, we are exposed to numerous approaches that focus on our ability to articulate and comprehend through verbalisation. In primary schools and early years settings, we have communication and spoken language skills embedded within each stage of the curriculum to ensure that we can measure the progress of each student. As we shift the focus into secondary schools, it is clear that there are still areas in which we need to alter the perception of oracy and its place in education.

In secondary schools, oracy has (in some circumstances) become subject specific. Although we implicitly engage with spoken language through reasoning and questioning of comprehension, there are no specific indicators that these skills are being developed unless their development is specified in an assessment-driven environment.

Yet, when we consider the significance of oracy, it is clear that the doors this skill can open are plentiful. The ability of high-performing students to articulate their capabilities in interviews; the ability of a struggling individual to verbalise their thoughts and feelings to others; the ability to develop a rapport through dialogue – all of these are possible when we engage with oracy and ensure it receives the time and recognition it deserves.

CONTRIBUTIONS

When I first embarked on the challenge of bringing more attention to oracy, I was keen to ensure that this publication featured a variety of voices that were able to share their own experiences of how they have adopted and developed strategies in their own settings. By providing realistic and reflective examples, each practitioner has provided a unique perspective that can hopefully be used to support your own oracy development.

Case Study 1: Oracy strategies that can be used through transition

Hydeh Fayaz is a year 5 teacher, lead practitioner and evidence lead of education at St Matthew's Primary School. She has written blogs for the Research School's website. St Matthew's CofE Primary School is a Teaching and Research school and Talk for Writing training centre.

Case Study 2: Oracy in key stage 5 science

Robert Murray-Green has taught A level chemistry for twelve years at two large 'outstanding' sixth form colleges. He has been a curriculum leader in chemistry for the last nine years, and has managed teaching both AQA and OCR A level chemistry specifications. Under his supervision, Robert's classes have a robust track record of achievement above all national averages. He also has a strong, online e-learning presence with a well-established YouTube channel of short tutorials. As a result of this, he was nominated for a sixth form college 'innovative teaching award' in 2018.

Case study 3: Oracy in geography

Jennifer Monk is currently head of geography at Golborne High School. She is a specialist leader of education (SLE) and is also a consultant to the Geographical Association. Jennifer has won an award from the Royal Geographical Society for her excellence in teaching secondary geography.

Case study 4: Oracy in the primary curriculum

Laura Baxter is an experienced teacher and English specialist at Woodlands Primary School in Birkenhead, where she is a member of the senior leadership team (SLT). With a background in drama and a masters in creative practice, she has always had an interest in oracy.

Case Study 5: A senior leader's perspective

Sam Strickland is the principal of a large all-through school and has helped to guide its GCSE results from the bottom 20% nationally to the top 20% and A level outcomes to the top 5% nationally. Sam began his teaching career as a history teacher in Bedfordshire, having completed his postgraduate certificate in education (PGCE) in secondary history at the University of Cambridge under Christine Counsell. His career quickly accelerated and he became head of history and classics. He then moved on to become a lead professional and worked for a SCITT (School Centred Initial Teacher Training) consortium. In 2015 Sam served as an associate principal, with GCSE and A level results under his tenure receiving commendation from the Department for Education (DfE), Nick Gibb and the SSAT (the Schools, Students and Teachers Network). Sam then served as a vice principal, where he directly oversaw student care, the sixth form and the curriculum, and served as the safeguarding lead for an entire trust. The organiser of ResearchED Northampton, he is a leading voice in the current conversation in education. He has had educational resources and research published and has delivered courses nationally.

Case study 6: Oracy in divinity

Marie Mulcrow has had numerous roles in her twenty years' experience of teaching that include head of year, spiritual leader in sixth form, second in department, progress leader, and head of department. She is currently working at Saint Martin's Catholic Academy.

Case Study 7: Using storytelling and drama in the classroom

Chris Connaughton is a children's author and playwright who tours extensively to primary schools with his storytelling performances and writing workshops. He is the author of The Beltheron series of fantasy thrillers for upper key stage 2 and key stage 3, and has had plays for young audiences commissioned by Theatre Hullabaloo, The Berry Theatre and Cleveland Theatre Company. As a professional actor, he has played many Shakespearean roles, as well as appearing in Byker Grove and on Button Moon! Info on his educational work and school visits can be found at intextperformance.com.

Case study 8: Raising the profile of oracy

Lucy Bellingham is a drama teacher, examiner and education consultant who has worked with schools, colleges and theatre companies in London and the midlands for the last 20 years. She is the founder of the company Teaching Drama (www. teachingdrama.org), which provides training and resources for secondary drama teachers.

Case study 9: Oracy in drama

In Wales, performing arts specialists like Zak Frost have been working on developing the implementation of oracy assessments through the implementation of a whole-school framework that is used in correlation with those embedded for literacy and numeracy.

Case study 10: Introducing oracy through leadership

Helen Mars holds a teaching and learning role in a high-achieving state grammar school in the north of England, and has been working with the literacy coordinator/head librarian to push the implementation and effective use of oracy in her setting.

Case Study 11: Oracy in history

Amanda Jacob is a history teacher and an assistant head teacher in a secondary school in Oldham. Her previous roles have been as an advanced skills teacher, head of humanities and head of history.

WHY FOCUS ON ORACY?

Make thyself a craftsman in speech, for thereby thou shalt gain the upper hand.

Inscription found in a 3000-year-old Egyptian tomb

It is hoped that the tips, support and reflections that are provided throughout this book can offer you an opportunity to develop an appreciation for embedding oracy skills in the curriculum. Before we embark on introducing these strategies and providing useful guidance, we must first consider the significance and the substantial life skills that underpin this approach. By considering a more intrinsic approach to the development of communication, we can help students in:

- post-16 academic interviews
- relationships in future employment
- future family and personal relationships.

All of these have something in common – they all require a substantial grasp of the effective use of oracy skills. The more students are exposed to these skills in their academic journeys, the more comfortable and competent they will feel when experiencing these scenarios in real life.

By tackling the stigma surrounding the explicit teaching of oracy skills in secondary schools and considering what effective strategies are being adopted in primary school settings, we can realistically begin to question why standards and expectations have not always been upheld as students transition through the key stages. Whereas we assume that there would be a natural trajectory and development path (as there are for literacy and numeracy), there are very few intrinsic markers post-early years that can support the assessment and mapping of development in communication.

When we consider the possibility that progress and development may have a direct correlation with the ability to comprehend and articulate interpretations, we can see that the foundations of knowledge acquisition are fundamentally spoken language skills. Consequently, it is possible to suggest that oracy skills act as the catalyst on which knowledge acquisition is founded.

According to the English-Speaking Union (ESU) and various other charities working to raise awareness of oracy skills in the classroom, the facts behind why this fundamental principle of learning needs to gain recognition include:

- Disadvantaged children are 2.3 times more likely to be identified as having speech, language and communication needs than are those in more affluent areas (The Communication Trust, 2015).

- In many parts of the country, over 50% of students start school lacking vital oracy skills (Lee, 2013).

- Young people who cannot express themselves verbally may suffer from behavioural problems and emotional and psychological difficulties and, in some cases, may descend into criminality (Owen).

- Some pupils in inner-city classes contribute on average just four words per lesson (National Literacy Trust, 2019).

- The UK's poorest children start school 19 months behind their wealthier peers in language and vocabulary (National Literacy Trust, 2019).

(Adapted from English-Speaking Union, 2020, with internal sources retained)

The same group then goes on to summarise the benefits of implementing a clear and concise approach to oracy within the classroom:

- High-quality spoken dialogue in primary classrooms can significantly improve children's educational attainment, from improving SAT results in maths and science to improving reading, writing and reasoning skills (The Communication Trust).

- Cognitively challenging classroom talk for children in year 5 not only improves their language skills, but can also lead to gains equivalent to about two months' additional progress in mathematics and science (Dialogic Teaching, Education Endowment Foundation).

- Oracy improves literacy, including reading comprehension, spelling and writing (LKMco & Voice 21).

- Spoken language plays a key role in cognitive development, helping children understand the world around them (LKMco & Voice 21).

- 97% of teachers, 94% of employers and 88% of young people believe that life skills such as confidence, motivation, resilience and communication are as or more important than academic qualifications (Sutton Trust).

- Evidence shows that oracy has a positive impact on academic and cognitive outcomes, self-esteem, wellbeing and mental health, social mobility, employability and civic engagement (Jay et al.; Hanley; Slavin and Elliot; Nagda and Gurin).

- Social and emotional learning (SEL), which debate, public speaking and cultural exchange all foster, appears to be particularly beneficial for disadvantaged or low-attaining pupils (Education Endowment Foundation).

(Adapted from ESU, 2020, with internal sources retained)

Even when we consider the substantial focus on the positive impact that implementation can have on learners, when researching oracy and dialogic teaching it is clear that the l focus has been on how these skills are acquired and developed in the primary years (ages 5–11). From a child development perspective, it's understandable why this is the key focus. However, it is how we then continue to nurture these skills that requires additional attention and consideration.

What are oracy skills?

The idea that spoken language has been relegated to a subject-specific curriculum is preposterous, though it is certainly the case in some establishments. It is undoubtedly an approach that may be overlooked if schools and colleges do not make a conscious effort to embed recognition and explicit teaching of fundamental principles of oracy and the importance of their transfer into the classroom into the whole-school ethos.

In 1999, Voice 21, alongside Oracy Cambridge, combined their expertise to create a clearer and more concise understanding of the holistic interpretation of oracy. They concluded that the framework of oracy skills should be divided into four key components:

- **Cognitive**
  - The concept of understanding what information is and how a response can be formulated in a manner that provides comprehension and understanding. Being able to develop and justify a point or interpretation enables a person to present more effective oracy skills.

23

- **Physical**

    - The art of communication isn't solely in the words that are spoken, but in how information is projected onto the audience. In order to consider a holistic overview, one must also appreciate and recognise how the voice and the body language of the contributor can have a substantial impact on the interpretation of concepts.

- **Linguistic**

    - This is all about the *How?* The way in which information is presented is just as vital as the intended message, but we're all aware of this, as this concept is one that is constantly reiterated in academia. Often our focus is on the ability to structure an extensive and perceptive written response that demonstrates our knowledge and understanding. What is often misplaced however, is how this can transcribe into oral communication. The art of rhetoric, as well as the presentation of factual and statistical information, is often misconstrued as a literacy concept. However, their linguistic purpose is just as important in regard to the way both techniques can actually support the structure and enhancement of effective communication.

- **Social and Emotional**

    - It is the ability to incorporate and embed these skills that will allow our learners to become more attentive and well-rounded individuals in the long run. The ability to recognise that communication needs to be a two-way street, alongside the skills to demonstrate awareness and attentiveness to an audience, are what will support the opportunity for success post-academia.

The Oracy Skills Framework and Glossary

Voice 21 (2019)

Oracy
Cambridge

The Hughes Hall Centre for Effective Spoken Communication

voice 21

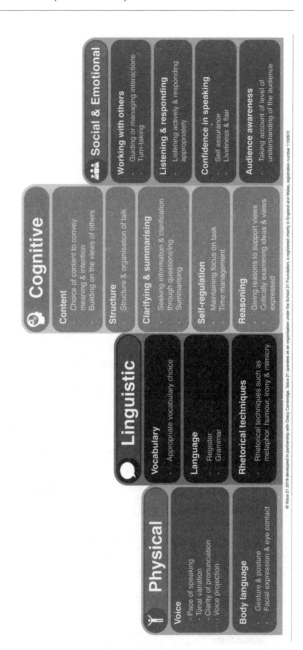

Physical

Voice
- Pace of speaking
- Tonal variation
- Clarity of pronunciation
- Voice projection

Body language
- Gesture & posture
- Facial expression & eye contact

Linguistic

Vocabulary
- Appropriate vocabulary choice

Language
- Register
- Grammar

Rhetorical techniques
- Rhetorical techniques such as metaphor, humour, irony & mimicry

Cognitive

Content
- Choice of content to convey meaning & intention
- Building on the views of others

Structure
- Structure & organisation of talk

Clarifying & summarising
- Seeking information & clarification through questioning
- Summarising

Self-regulation
- Maintaining focus on task
- Time management

Reasoning
- Giving reasons to support views
- Critically examining ideas & views expressed

Social & Emotional

Working with others
- Guiding or managing interactions
- Turn-taking

Listening & responding
- Listening actively & responding appropriately

Confidence in speaking
- Self assurance
- Liveliness & flair

Audience awareness
- Taking account of level of understanding of the audience

© Voice 21 2019 developed in partnership with Oracy Cambridge. Voice 21 operates as an organisation under the School 21 Foundation, a registered charity in England and Wales, registration number 1152672

This information can be adapted into a crib sheet of questions that students and practitioners alike can utilise in order to approach the effective implementation of these skills.

Composite	Component	Comments
Physical Skills	Voice *Are they audible?* *Is there a variation in their tone?* *Is there a clarity in pronunciation?*	
	Body Language *Describe their posture and any gestures.* *Are they able to make eye contact?*	
Linguistic Skills	Vocabulary *Have they used sophisticated vocabulary?* *Is their vocabulary choice suited to purpose?*	
	Language *Have they used any rhetorical devices?* *What is the intention of these?*	
Cognitive skills	Content *Does the speech convey meaning and intention?* *Is the speech interesting and fact based?* *Has the speech been structured for clarity?*	
	Summarising *Is there a clear summary to the speech?*	
	Reasoning *Does the speech maintain focus on the topic?* *Are reasons provided to support the viewpoint?* *Are ideas critically examined?*	
Social and Emotional Skills	Confidence in speaking *Is confidence being presented by the speaker?* *Is the speaker active with visual cues?*	
	Audience Awareness *Does the speaker maintain eye contact?* *Is there an awareness of and address to the audience?*	

Having recognised the components of oracy, it is then the responsibility of the school and its practitioners to ensure that the approach is being adopted and utilised to its full potential. The encouragement of oracy can be assessed based on the oracy benchmarks that were outlined as part of Voice 21's research into skills implementation. It is suggested that for these skills to become embedded to the extent of mastery, a school must:

- have an ambitious vision for oracy.
- build a culture of oracy.
- have a sustained and wide-ranging curriculum for oracy.
- recognise oracy as central to learning.
- be accountable for the impact of oracy.

Consequently, it is the requirement that teachers should:

- set high standards for oracy.
- value every voice.
- teach oracy explicitly.
- harness oracy to elevate learning.
- appraise progress of oracy.

Through the adoption of these benchmarks, establishments can begin to appreciate the extent of the impact that oracy can have on an individual's ability to achieve their full potential.

The significance of child development

When we consider the origin of communication, the attention needs to be on how we would expect children to develop into socially functioning adults. The need to communicate is one of the first skills that babies attempt from birth. They cry when they are hungry, tired, uncomfortable, in pain, or in need of close physical contact with a caregiver. They laugh when they are happy and yawn when they are tired. Infants may not be able to hold a conversation or articulate their needs in words, but through the use of body language, facial expressions and sounds, they can make you completely aware of a particular need.

It is from this young age that we see the emergence of two different sets of communication skills that will form the basis for their future development:

Receptive communication is the ability to use vocalisation to acknowledge the comprehension and receipt of a message from another person. Although at the start this vocalisation could be a simple 'coo' or another sound, the response indicates understanding.

Expressive communication is the ability to convey a message to others. No matter what the form of communication (babble, crying, body language), this is the key first step to effective communication.

The fact of the matter is that survival relies heavily on the ability to communicate. No matter what form this takes in later life, our development depends to a significant extent on the ability to share and acquire information (particularly when we are in our most vulnerable infantile state).

Age	Receptive language	Expressive Language
1 2	• The ability to listen to and follow simple commands. • Interaction through acknowledgement and pointing. • The ability to use gestures to communicate (including responding to yes or no questions). • Listening to and responding to simple questions.	• Can assimilate up to 50 words. • Able to combine words to create simple phrases.
3	• Able to follow two-step commands. • Can identify actions whilst demonstrating the ability to comprehend prepositions.	• Child has now acquired between 200 and 500 intelligible words. • Can answer simple questions and is able to respond using up to three words in phrases whilst incorporating pronouns.
4	• The child is able to follow three-step commands (although we know from experience that this can be quite difficult even for an older child!). • Now, the child has begun to comprehend more contrasting concepts, with the ability to formulate a more developed response.	• Now able to combine words in order to create simple sentences (usually around four to five words). • Begins to show an ability to incorporate more complex sentences into their dialogue. • Is beginning to demonstrate an ability to recollect in chronological order by sequencing two consecutive events.
5	• The child becomes able to demonstrate basic comprehension to a reader/response situation. • They are able to distinguish even more contrasting concepts.	• Able to produce interrogative statements that demonstrate questioning and knowledge acquisition. • Able to articulate a narrative of events to another person. For example, the child will be able to provide brief details about their day in chronological order.
6	• Able to understand contrasting concepts associated with the same topic.	• States similarities and differences between objects.

It is from this point that a child then enters full-time education. This is where the ability to communicate is more explicitly managed and enabled to progress through the incorporation of oracy as a process embedded into the curriculum. Recognition that this knowledge is acquired as opposed to innate is predominantly centred around cognitive development theory.

Understanding cognitive development theory

Piaget's perspective argues that children are active participants in their learning and understanding. Piaget proposed that adaptation through observation and interaction is a contributing factor to our ability to survive. While one could dispute or counteract some of Piaget's interpretation and definitive approach, there is some clear rationality in the suggestion that human beings MUST learn how to communicate for basic survival needs:

> Intelligence is something that grows and develops through a series of stages. Older children do not just think more quickly than younger children, [Piaget] suggested. Instead, there are both qualitative and quantitative differences between the thinking of young children versus older children. (Cherry, 2020)

How this can be linked to the necessity for oracy relates to the concept that older children are able to rationalise their initial reflections in a way that demonstrates a more articulated response or interpretation. Entry into what Piaget referred to as the 'formal operational stage' allows children to demonstrate logic alongside consideration of abstract concepts in detail. When we consider some of the key characteristics of this stage (Piaget referred to those aged twelve and up), we must also consider how we can relate these to communication:

- the ability to think abstractly and conduct hypothetical reasoning
- the consideration of more moral, philosophical, social and political issues that require reasoning
- the ability to incorporate deductive logic and reasoning.

The suggestion is that promoting the development of these communication skills leads to the development of an internal dialogue that can be used to support knowledge acquisition and consideration. Vygotsky, cited in Britton (1993), refers to this as 'speech for oneself'. This process of internalised language is essential for problem-solving, reasoning and abstract thinking skills. This implies that an inability to internalise language consequently has a detrimental impact on the cognitive development of the individual. Early infant and carer interaction is essential for all areas of a child's development. As a child's language develops, they go from talking in the present tense alone to including the past and future tenses. Piaget suggests that not until a child has learned the concept of time will this be displayed within their language use.

Considering the intricacy and necessity of the development of communication skills in the early years allows us to reflect on the extent to which these skills are acquired and developed within the early stages of education.

The question that practitioners then need to consider is whether our perception of the acquisition of these skills has allowed us to become complacent in our explicit acknowledgement of oracy within the curriculum and in the classroom. Our understanding that by the time students leave their primary school they are able to justify, reason and rationalise through language almost acts as a deterrent to the idea that these theories might require further development through discussion and elaboration.

Having accepted the amount of time and effort that goes into studying the ability to communicate in the earlier years of child development, what we then need to do is continue that trajectory in all educational establishments in order to retain children's ability and continue the projected evolution of these skills.

CASE STUDY 1 – ORACY STRATEGIES THAT CAN BE USED THROUGH TRANSITION

Hydeh Fayaz is a year 5 teacher, lead practitioner and evidence lead of education at St Matthew's Primary School. She has written blogs for the Research Schools website. St Matthew's CofE Primary School is a Teaching and Research school and Talk for Writing training centre.

St Matthew's is a primary school in Nechells – one of the poorest areas of Birmingham and amongst the most deprived neighbourhoods in the country (2019). Through evidence-informed practice, the team at St Matthew's strives to provide our pupils with an ambitious, knowledge-rich curriculum which reflects the diverse community and world in which they live.

Emphasis is placed on building reciprocal relationships with our pupils; we as a school want to learn from the child, their family, their culture and heritage and tap into the 'funds of knowledge' held by our community and the families within it (Gonzales, 2006). The two-way learning street that is ever flourishing at St Matthew's relies on the ability of our children to express themselves. Sonia Thompson, the head teacher, shares her vision for the children of our school:

> We want to open doors for our children and we want them to step through these with confidence into a future world where they will hopefully make a huge difference (Thompson 2020).

In a time where multiple distractions exist outside of education, we continuously refer back to Daniel Willingham's assertion that 'memory is the residue of thought' (Willingham, 2009). If we want our children to remember the knowledge learnt in the classroom, then they must actively think about what they are being taught. An environment in which children co-create critical thoughts through talk is what we aim for.

Empowering our children through talk and the curriculum is what will make them successful. Lauren Resnick states that in order for the full development of student capacities and dispositions for reasoned civic participation (Resnick et al., 2010), students need to be immersed in accountable talk, a Vygostskian theoretical framework which stresses the 'social formation of the mind', talk which is:

1. accountable to the community

2. accountable to standards of reasoning

3. accountable to knowledge.

Below are a collection of examples demonstrating how we ensure oracy is developed in all parts of the curriculum.

Our pupils' talk is *accountable to the community* in whole-class, shared reading. At St Matthew's, we have a holistic approach to ensure our children are successful readers who want to read. Based on Doug Lemov's 'close reading strategies', our whole class reads from an ambitious text (whether that be poetry, non-fiction or fiction), giving pupils the opportunity to 'attend seriously and build on the ideas of others' (Lemov et al., 2016). Navigated by the teacher, pupils are encouraged to build on their peers' ideas and must work to unpick which response is most accurate, thinking about the text and the background information needed to truly grapple with and understand it.

This practice of verbalising ideas in reading is to ensure that discussions are effective and that they support the ability to consider alternative viewpoints and perspectives on a topic. The habits of discussion in reading are intended to ensure our pupils gain a deeper understanding of what they are reading. This means that students who have an incorrect answer must tune into the correct **understanding** and amend their responses. The fluid nature of talk which occurs in shared reading can be identified as 'exploratory talk' (Gaunt and Stott, 2019), where pupils are praised for changing their mind based on the evidence presented. Using the habits of discussion also allows our pupils to practise the key habits of reading, e.g. clarifying (Tennent et al., 2016).

Habit	Description	Sentence Starters
Paraphrase or clarify	• Ask clarifying questions of each other • Rephrase and refine other students' ideas • Test the logic • Repeat and add on, build on students' answers • Provide evidence and examples	• 'So what you're saying is...' • 'I think what _____ meant was...' • 'Are you saying that...?' • 'What _____ is saying is ... and I agree/disagree because...' • 'I agree with _____ about _____ because...'

Habits of Discussion when reading – adapted from Doug Lemov et al. (2016)

Once the discussions have concluded and notes have been captured, pupils will then form a written response in order to 'use writing as a tool to refine and develop their informal thoughts' (Lemov et al., 2016). The collaborative, reciprocal nature of the discussion is crucial for pupils to begin to understand the 'Art of the Sentence' when writing.

Possible Independent Practice

but, so, because

'The Anglo-Saxons were originally pagans.'

e.g.

The Anglo-Saxons were originally pagans but converted to Christianity in around AD 597.

The Anglo-Saxons were originally pagans because the religions in their homelands were polytheistic.

The Anglo-Saxons were originally pagans so they worshipped lots of gods.

The Art of the Sentence in action using the Hochman method in *The Writing Revolution*

The pupils at St Matthew's are *accountable to the standards of reasoning* in maths, whereby reasoning and problem-solving are explicitly modelled before the children have a go. Key talk frames are provided at the initial stages of learning so that children can express themselves and adopt the language of reasoning and problem-solving early on in concrete stages of the concept. Using reasoning tools such as 'Convince me' or 'If I know then I know' in the concrete stages allows children to not only understand procedural knowledge but to experience 'cognitive work that poses moderate challenge' (Willingham, 2009) in a high challenge, low threat way. As Neil Mercer states, 'ways of thinking are embedded in ways of using language' (Mercer and Littleton, 2007). This is why talking frames are crucial at the very beginning of a new concept, as they lay the groundwork for a written or more sophisticated response later on.

Represent

123,405

27,421

Can you order them from smallest to greatest?

If I know _____ then I know

This number is >/< because

100000s	10000s	1000s	100s	10s	1s
100000 100000	10000		100	10	1
			100		1
					1
					1

An example of talk frames in the Represent stage during the Place Value unit in Y4

Our pupils' talk is *accountable to knowledge* in history – a subject in which the validity and reliability of sources must be evaluated – a wider skill that is more vital now than ever in a world filled with fake news and misinformation. Talk around the validity of sources is effective because pupils are exposed to the background information via shared reading, a knowledge organiser, or explicit teaching and revisiting of the facts required in order to critique a historical source, or an enquiry question.

The figure below provides an example of planned modelling and scaffolds, so children can practise the skill of asking clarifying questions when prompted with a secondary historical source (Quigley, 2018).

Teaching how to generate questions through modelling examples based on enquiry

(Stems: Who, When, Where, Why, How, Why on board)

My Turn (MT) - who might be in this picture (modal verb *might* for degree of certainty)?

MT - Why is the little boy wearing red (example of question that isn't going to support our answer to the enquiry)

Model rewording it about the little boy's clothes -

Why is the little boy wearing clothes that are torn and dirty, when the man in the middle is very well dressed?)

Your Turn - T and TA to tune in on specific pairs

Feedback using Quigley's ABC response

Vocabulary in context:
Mercy:
Overseer:

Source B: 'Just starve us', comic and song, words by W.H. Freeman, music by Auber.
Published: 1843, London

Summarise your discussion and what you have deduced from this image.
We have deduced that

_____

Does the information from Source A match the suggestion made in Source B?

Yes	No

Not only do we develop the children's cognitive and linguistic ability to speak, we want to build their physical, social and emotional strands. To do this we reference the Oracy Framework created by Cambridge University and teachers at School 21. The Education Endowment Fund's guidance on meta-cognition states that: 'Explicit instruction in cognitive and metacognitive strategies can improve pupils' learning' (Quigley et al., 2018). So, as teachers, we ensure that we model habits in our children's subconscious and clearly state our learning focus so that children can self-assess and improve across all strands of the Oracy Framework.

Vocabulary Instruction across the curriculum

In order for our pupils' talk to be:

1. accountable to the community

2. accountable to standards of reasoning

3. accountable to knowledge...

We at St Matthew's know that vocabulary underpins purposeful talk. Cultivating vocabulary is the way to enrich what the children are saying. We understand that [our] efforts, in delivering robust vocabulary instruction ... can advance children's access to the curriculum' (Quigley, 2018). As Beck et al. maintain:

> Learning words well enough to express them is an important learning goal, and having words in one's productive vocabulary is a good measure of word ownership (Beck et al., 2013).

We want to raise the quality of talk, and in order to do this must ensure our children have the range of vocabulary needed to immerse themselves in the different ways of talking which Robin Alexander so brilliantly explores in *A Dialogic Teaching Companion* (Alexander, 2018). Tier 2 and 3 Vocabulary in all its contexts is explicitly taught and practised in daily vocabulary sessions which allow children to understand nuances in vocabulary such as the parameters of words or how they are used in different contexts.

Word	Definition	My association	Reasons/ explanations
Scarcely			
Dim			
Revive/-ing/-ed			
Nestle			
Reluctantly			

An activity taken from Isabel Beck's *Bringing Words to Life* with Tier 2 vocabulary in an extract from 'Mementos' by Charlotte Bronte, a Y5 unit taken from Bob Cox's *Opening Doors to Quality Writing*.

INCLUSION IN ORACY

The concept of inclusion is one that needs to be considered and effectively implemented by every practitioner. It is the responsibility of those facilitating groups of individuals to ensure that all students are provided with a fair and consistent education, allowing access to the same opportunities and approaches as those offered to their peers.

No matter how you choose to approach the concept of oracy in the classroom, it is important to recognise that your strategies must be accessible to all of your learners. To do this, you must first have a grasp of your cohort and their abilities.

We need to establish that barriers to learning should not be perceived as limitations to learning, and that learning should never be restricted, but should be adapted where necessary to provide an alternative route to the end goal. A crucial role of every practitioner is ensuring the right of all students to an inclusive education.

The United Nations specifies that the concept of an inclusive education refers to:

- a fundamental right to education
- a principle that values students' wellbeing, dignity, autonomy, and contribution to society
- a continuing process to eliminate barriers to education and promote reform in the culture, policy, and practice in schools to include all students.

(UNESCO, 2017)

The 2017 Guide for Ensuring Inclusion and Equity in Education focusses on the key dimensions of ensuring inclusive and equitable education systems:

Concepts	1.1	Inclusion and equity are overarching principles that guide all education policies, plans and practices.
	1.2	The national curriculum and its associated assessment systems are designed to respond effectively to all learners.
	1.3	All partners who work with learners and their families understand and support the national policy goals for promoting inclusion and equity in education.
	1.4	Systems are in place to monitor the presence, participation, and achievement of all learners within the education system.
Policy	2.1	The important national education policy documents strongly emphasise inclusion and equity.
	2.2	Senior staff at the national, district, and school levels provide leadership on inclusion and equity in education.
	2.3	Leaders at all levels articulate consistent policy goals to develop inclusion and equitable educational practices.
	2.4	Leaders at all levels challenges non-inclusive, discriminatory and inequitable educational practices.
Structures and Systems	3.1	There is high-quality support for vulnerable learners.
	3.2	All services and institutions involved with learners and their families work together in coordinating inclusive and equitable educational policies and practices.
	3.3	Resources, both human and financial, are distributed in ways that benefit potentially vulnerable learners.
	3.4	There is a clear role for special provision, such as special schools and units, in promoting inclusion and equity in education.
Practices	4.1	Schools and other learning centres have strategies for encouraging the presence, participation, and achievement of all learners from their local community and have opportunities to take part in continuing professional development regarding inclusive and equitable practices.
	4.2	Schools and other learning centres provide support for learners who are at risk of underachievement, marginalisation, and exclusion.
	4.3	Teachers and support staff are prepared to respond to learner diversity during their initial training.
	4.4	Teachers and support staff have opportunities to take part in continuing professional development regarding inclusive and equitable practices.

(Schuelka, 2018)

From a classroom-specific perspective, this requirement for inclusivity is based on the consideration of three key components. These are:

- **Teaching styles**

  The variety of teaching styles that have been introduced over the years can be overwhelming. What is important is that we take our audience into consideration prior to the learning taking place. Although certain adaptations may not be appropriate in a larger cohort (assemblies, lecture theatres, etc.), effective communication can often be built on a degree of rapport. This includes the incorporation by the practitioner of suitable strategies to account for contextualisation and situational analysis.

- **Learning objectives**

  The learning objectives (not to be mistaken for learning outcomes) are commonly summarised as what the learner has either learned or achieved by the end of a lesson/presentation or unit of study. It is vital in an inclusive learning environment that this learning objective is accessible to all. This ensures that all students are accessing a mainstream education whilst still receiving a curriculum that is suitably adapted for any additional needs that they may have – offering a bespoke but inclusive learning opportunity for all.

- **Access to learning**

  All students have a right to access learning, and anything that impedes this needs to be considered, with preventative action taking place. There are several factors that can impede a student's learning, and these include:

  - special educational needs
  - English as an additional language
  - gender
  - age
  - culture or religious beliefs.

According to Tanenbaum, there are seven principles that must be considered to achieve inclusion for all learners. These are:

- the provision to teach all students
- the opportunity to explore multiple identities
- the prevention of prejudice

- the promotion of social justice
- the ability to choose appropriate materials
- teaching and learning about different cultures and religions
- the ability to adapt and integrate into lessons appropriately.

(Tanenbaum, 2016)

It is only when an establishment begins to demonstrate how these three components are carefully considered in all situations that an educational setting can begin to refer to itself as inclusive for all.

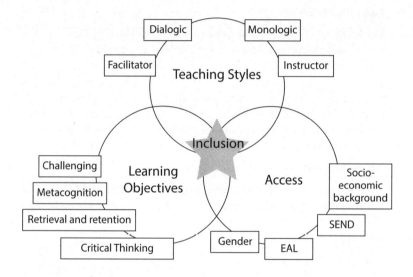

It is through the effective implementation of oracy strategies and an explicit teaching of oracy that we can support the inclusion of those who may have previously been unable to access a broad and balanced curriculum to the same degree as their peers. Through communication development, we can begin to acknowledge new doors and learning opportunities that are available to all learners.

Oracy and special educational needs and disabilities (SEND)

Since 2014, the SEND code of practice has outlined statutory guidance regarding the legal duties of organisations that interact with young people with special educational needs and/or disabilities.

In light of this, The Communication Trust introduced its supporting documentation for this code of practice, which it referred to as *Communicating the Code*. Throughout this document, The Communication Trust outlines and provides additional information to support the implementation of effective strategies that can be used with learners who may require additional support or guidance.

Recognising that there are different types of special educational needs, it is important to possess an appreciation and awareness of how each individual student can be provided with a bespoke learning approach that is suited to their individual requirements.

There are many inhibiting factors that may prove to be barriers for the development of coherent communication and the explicit development of oracy skills. The 2008 Bercow review used the term 'Speech, Language and Communication needs' (SLCN) to distinguish between the inhibiting factors for children or young people who may require support. The term SLCN accounts for those individuals for whom communication may bring with it additional difficulties. These difficulties include:

- where there is a specific language impairment that may serve as the primary need in the absence of any other issues
- where SLCN difficulties are the by-products of the effects of other conditions that can include autism, deafness or cerebral palsy
- the result of a social and/or environmental disadvantage.

(Bercow, 2008, p. 6)

It is vital to understand and appreciate these issues in order to recognise the impact of SLCN in today's society. To accompany next change, The Communication Trust estimated that in 2013 around 10% of all children had persistent and long-term SLCN (The Communication Trust, 2014).

In light of the various developmental tests that are performed as a child enters primary school, SLCNs are often picked up once a child enters key stage 1. However, it is not uncommon for these issues to be missed, as they are often difficult to recognise. As a result, students can go through academia with underlying SLCN issues that could have been identified, supported and perhaps even improved through the correct implementation and development of oracy skills.

No matter what your audience, it is helpful to look out for signs and indicators that there may be some underlying reason behind ineffective communication. These can include:

- demonstrating a difficulty in taking turns in conversation
- demonstrating an inability to initiate conversation
- general anger and frustration when attempting to articulate
- poor social skills
- speech that is difficult to understand and may be inaudible
- difficulty in comprehending what is being said
- inability to follow instructions and understand the tasks that have been set
- immature vocabulary use that may appear simplified or not appropriate for the age.

What is significant about a number of these signs is that they are commonly associated with negative or deviant behaviour. The frustration and aggression that can sometimes be exhibited by a student could actually derive from the student's inability to articulate their issues, in the same (although slightly crude) way a toddler has a tantrum because they are frustrated with the fact that they cannot tell you what they want or need.

These situations can be approached in a way that provides support and guidance through the conversations that take place between the practitioner and the learner. By putting more vocal ownership of strategies and approaches onto the individuals, the code of practice began the process that most schools now refer to as student 'passports'. This is the result of the specification that establishments have a responsibility to ensure that:

Consulting with, and enabling participation of, the child or young person is part of all aspects of the SEND process and as well as informing support for the individual should also influence SEND systems such as the Local Offer and Joint Commissioning. (The Communication Code, p. 10)

What this statement suggests is that it is vital that individuals contribute to and communicate with agencies about how best to proceed with their own care and education of others. This process is also encouraged as part of developing documentation that can support those adults who may interact with the young person.

Questions that could be asked in these discussions include:

- What do you enjoy doing in your spare time?
- What would you like your teacher to know about you?
- What causes you to lose focus on your learning?
- What can teachers do to support you?
- What can you do that will help yourself?
- What do you find difficult?
- What do you enjoy?

This information can then be collected and distributed to relevant staff members (as well as being retained in a central database), alongside any additional information that may need to be acknowledged, such as the support that students receive in lessons or any access arrangements that have been put in place for assessments and examinations.

Introducing this through a discussion supports the interpretation of the outcome being formed by all parties involved. By allowing the learner to drive the support, the sense of ownership in most cases can reduce any negative or deviant behaviour that could have been avoided had these support needs been identified sooner. Of course, this isn't always going to be the case. Negative behaviour should not be deemed inevitable, but rather perceived as arising from a situation with a variety of variables that can affect the outcomes of that situation. The knowledge and information gathered during these primary discussions will therefore form the foundations of support.

When introducing this strategy, there are, of course, factors that need to be taken into consideration so that communication can truly be the foundation of successful outcomes for each individual. These issues include:

- The need for a skilled practitioner to participate in the conversation so that the objective is met and all areas are covered
- The need for time to be allocated for these interactions to happen, with the conversation being promoted as one that can be developed and considered as opposed to rushed and poorly scheduled with inconvenient meeting times
- Consideration of innovative techniques in order to communicate, given the nature of the difficulties faced by these learners

- The often distinct correlation between SCLN and reading or writing difficulties when communication issues are not picked up early enough

- The importance of limiting the perception of the parent as a proxy voice when dealing with learners who are able to articulate their feelings. There needs to be a holistic, shared vision for the learner; however, it is vital that this includes the individual's thoughts and feelings, and these can sometimes be muffled or constrained by parental involvement.

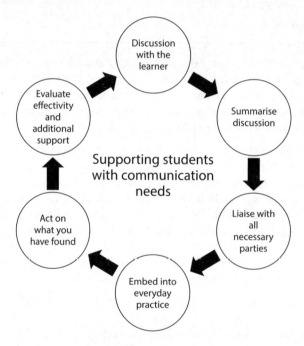

Making the whole process a shared dialogue between all agencies or parties involved promotes a clear, consistent and transparent approach that will promote reflection, evaluation and open communication.

Supporting students with English as an additional language (EAL)

According to the Bell Foundation, there are currently 1.5 million learners in UK maintained schools (and many more independent schools) who use English as an additional language. To condense this even further, this is equivalent to 21% of learners in the primary school population and 17% of those who attend secondary school (the Bell Foundation, 2018).

In order to provide a more geographical interpretation of the EAL distribution, Daniel Clark published findings based on the percentage of school students in 2018 whose first language is known (or believed to be) a language other than English (Clark, 2020).

Region	Primary School	Secondary School
Inner London	54.4%	49.7%
Outer London	46.8%	36.2%
West Midlands	22.9%	16.6%
Yorkshire and the Humber	18.3%	12.7%
North West	16.4%	10.4%
East Midlands	16.2%	10.4%
East of England	16%	10.2%
South East	15%	10.1%
South West	8.7%	5%
North East	7.8%	4.9%

This table presents a clear indication that a large proportion of students within our care do not see English as their primary language of communication. As a result, substantial steps need to be taken to ensure that these learners comprehend English. As with any variant, it is also important to recognise factors that need to be taken into consideration when providing an inclusive education to EAL learners. No two cases are the same. Just as it is important to open channels of communication where there are SCLN difficulties, so too must the process be undertaken to uncover as much supportive information as possible from any new arrival students.

Differentiating factors to take into account could include:

- Taking into consideration the parents' ability to speak English and whether or not English is spoken on a daily basis.

- The reasoning behind the move to the UK – for some this may have been for professional relocation; others could be refugees who have fled from war or persecution.

- The educational background of the learner prior to their arrival to the UK – for some students this may be their first experience of this form of education system; however, international schools have become more prevalent in the past ten years, providing a high calibre of English-speaking education.

- Recognition of the learner's academic ability – it may be that the learner is actually a highly able, talented individual. Recognition should not be confined specifically to a student's ability in subjects learned through English. It could be that the individual is extremely talented at a subject when studying it in their first language. Alternatively, it could be that the learner has underlying special educational needs that may not have been acknowledged, as they were hidden behind a failure to communicate.

- By taking into consideration social class and economic background, we can assess which learners may have faced substantial discrimination or poverty.

These factors, alongside the consideration of religious belief, support networks, and students' general experience of life in the UK, can all play a significant role in the ability of each student to communicate and thrive in a mainstream, English-speaking environment.

To put it into the perspective of the students, consider what they might be feeling on a day-to-day basis in a large educational setting.

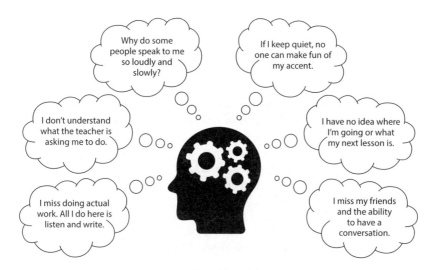

The development of oracy skills is crucial to the ability of EAL students to interact and to comprehend the English language. The more exposure they have to the dialect and how certain words or phrases are pronounced, the faster the rate of development in their own ability. There are a series of initial assessments and observations that can be conducted by an experienced practitioner to provide an understanding of the correct way to proceed with integration for each individual student. This approach includes:

- An initial meeting that takes place with the parents and the learner. It may be necessary for a translator to be present (for either or both parties), and this meeting is typically conducted by the EAL lead. It is during this time that basic information is collected, including:

  - time in the country

  - previous educational settings

  - language(s) spoken at home.

- After this meeting, a basic assessment can be conducted with the learner in order to develop an understanding of current capabilities. This assessment can obviously vary based on the statements collected during the initial conversation (international school attendees may require a more detailed assessment to support possible setting as opposed to proficiency). These assessments are there to provide a baseline assessment of the learner's capabilities in:

- listening and understanding
- speaking
- reading
- writing.

- This information is then collated, and a DfE proficiency code is allocated (see table). This proficiency grade, along with a summative report, should then be sent to all necessary teachers, alongside information on whether or not the student will qualify for any access arrangements and be supported with their mainstream integration. In most schools, students who obtain either a Code A or Code B are provided with more of an alternative provision for certain subjects to promote rapid development before being fully blended into mainstream. This provision (and the general development of EAL language acquisition) can be supported through approaches such as:

- more one-to-one verbal communication that can also be quite demonstrative in supporting comprehension
- collaborative learning opportunities in small peer groups, encouraging the use of English to communicate
- providing models and image supports that can be used to develop students' comprehension of subject-specific vocabulary
- providing opportunities to develop communication verbally before being asked to write anything down.

The Department of Education's EAL learner proficiency codes for oracy skills are presented below (DfE, 2016)

EAL Learner (DFE proficiency)	EAL Stage	Listening and Understanding	Speaking
New to English (Code A)	Step 1	Understands home language Watches and joins in routines/activities Follows instructions using key words/gestures Follows short sequences of instructions	Silent period Speaks in home language Non-verbal gesture Echoes words/expressions Simple naming vocabulary Basic, formulaic spoken exchanges Unclear pronunciation
	Step 2		

EAL Learner (DFE proficiency)	EAL Stage	Listening and Understanding	Speaking
Early Acquisition (Code B)	Step 3	Can indicate when they need to hear something again Listens attentively during lessons	Simple questions, e.g. where? Over-generalisation of grammatical rules Simple positional language
	Step 4	Understands function of time connectives Understands some teacher questions with visual support	Retells a simple story Can give a sequence of instructions Past simple tense emerging
Developing Competence (Code C)	Step 5	Follows set of oral instructions Differentiates past/future/present Begins to engage with how?	Speaks in simple everyday exchanges Uses common colloquialisms Uses extended sentences
	Step 6	and why? questions. Active listener asking for clarification Follows gist of teacher talk with limited visual support	Uses relative clauses Can contribute to whole-class discussion Plurals, articles, pronouns and prepositions
Competent (Code D)	Step 7	Shows understanding of the detail of curriculum topics with limited visuals Understands some idioms and phrasal verbs Beginning to understand inference Follows reasoning/discussion/argument	Uses the passive tense Communicates meaning – complex ideas/concepts Can express higher order thinking Moderates response according to listener
Fluent (Code E)	Step 8	Understanding is commensurate with that of a native English speaker Pupils have the range of listening skills required to participate fully in the National Curriculum for English	Variety of articles and prepositions used accurately Confident, fluent speech for multiple purposes/audiences Complex sentences used Accent does not interfere with understanding

Depending on the level of exposure to English, and based on their previous educational settings and the variety of factors that were identified at the start, it typically takes between five to seven years for EAL learners to become fluent in a language.

Obviously, this is dependent on the previously outlined factors, but this is a significant point to take into account when you consider that access arrangements for GCSE and other academic qualifications are only applicable to those students who have been in the country for less than three years, a period of time that could potentially be just on the cusp of 'developing competence' in the English language.

The specifics behind granting access arrangements for students have been outlined in detail by the Joint Council for Qualifications (JCQ) as specifying that, in order to access a bilingual dictionary, alongside 10% extra time, the centre must provide evidence of the following:

- the candidate's first language is not English, Irish or Welsh
- the candidate entered the UK within three years of the examination(s) with no prior knowledge of the English Language
- English is not one of the languages spoken in the family home
- prior to their arrival in the UK the candidate was not educated in an international school where some or the entire curriculum was delivered in English
- prior to their arrival in the UK the candidate was not prepared for or entered for IGCSE qualifications where the question papers were set in English
- prior to their arrival in the UK the candidate was not prepared in English for other qualifications, e.g. IELTS qualifications, Preliminary English Tests
- the candidate has to refer to the bilingual translation dictionary so often that examination time is used for this purpose, delaying the answering of questions
- the provision of 10% extra time reflects the candidate's usual way of working with the dictionary.

(adapted from Joint Council for Qualifications, 2020)

Given the thorough and rigorous process that exam centres have to go through to obtain access arrangements of this type, it is often complicated to prove that the candidate has fulfilled all of the criteria specified by the JCQ, particularly when you take into account that approximately 20% of the world's inhabitants have some capability in speaking English. There is also the rise in international schools across the world to consider when assessing a student's exposure to English. According to the International Baccalaureate programme, as of 14 July 2020 there were 7002 programmes being offered by international schools worldwide, covering 158 countries in total (International Baccalaureate, 2020).

	Number		% change	% of candidates taking exams	
Type of arrangement	2017/18	2018/19		2017/18 cohort	2018/19 cohort
25% extra time	235,105	256,710	▲ 9.2%	17.9	19.4
Computer reader/ reader	95,795	95,570	▼ 0.2%	7.3	7.2
Scribe/speech recognition technology	41,075	41,255	▲ 0.4%	3.1	3.1
Extra time over 25%	5,190	5,300	▲ 2.1%	0.4	0.4
Bilingual dictionary with extra time	2,905	2,450	▼ 15.7%	0.2	0.2
Other arrangements	11,115	3,315	▼ 70.2%	-	-
Total	391,185	404,600	▲ 3.4%	-	-

Department for Education (2018)

What is quite interesting when we consider these requirements for obtaining access arrangements during assessments is that the number of requests granted for centres has actually decreased by a substantial amount in the past few years.

Suggestions to explain this decrease include the possibility that:

- centres have instead chosen to recommend these students for 25% extra time instead of requesting access to a bilingual dictionary
- the rise in independent and international schools has allowed more people to access the English language prior to their arrival in the UK.

The fact is that there is a broad range of ability in students for whom English is considered an additional language. It is important to note that, even prior to taking into account any extenuating factors regarding personal circumstances, students' first language can prove to have a detrimental impact on their rate of progression, with particular regard to both their oracy and literacy skills, because the phonemes and lexicology demanded in the English language may differ so much from those of their first language.

An attainment gap has been identified by the Bell Foundation, which responded to the 2018 Multi-Academy Trust performance indicators in retaliation against its narrow average attainment gap regarding EAL students:

Figure 17: Average Attainment 8 score by pupil characteristics
England, state-funded schools, 2018

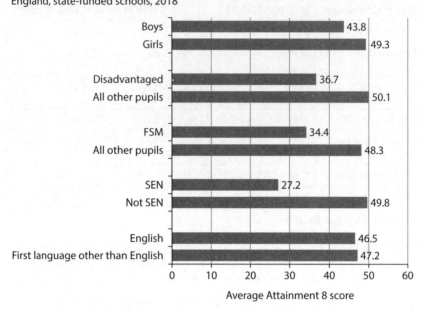

Average Attainment 8 score

Department for Education (2018)

The Bell Foundation stressed:

> The aggregated figures for learners who use English as an Additional Language (EAL) mask the real picture about the performance of EAL learners and the data hides as much as it tells us about students who speak another language at home. This is because the EAL indicator is a binary measure that defines the learner as 'any pupil that speaks a language in addition to English at home'.

The term EAL therefore covers a vastly different group of students, from advanced bilingual learners to those new to English, and whilst advanced bilinguals typically do outperform certain first language pupils once proficiency in English is achieved (for example Pashto and Turkish speakers), those arriving late into the English school system, those who have had poor prior education, and pupils who are new to English or below competency are all left behind (Bell, 2019).

What the research of the Bell Foundation alludes to is that many establishments can often be ill-prepared to support EAL students, particularly if they have not considered all of the contributing factors to students' ability and rate of progress. The implementation of effective oracy skills not only provides a provisional assessment in these situations, but can also assist in developing students' skills in language acquisition.

Strategies to promote oracy with EAL learners

When initial assessments have been conducted and a specific proficiency level has been determined, necessary interventions and support can be applied. Provisionally, the primary target is to provide students with the ability to access their lessons and comprehend the content to a specific degree. It is important that students are integrated into mainstream education so that they can develop their communication skills and access academia. However, we must first ensure that the foundations are strong enough to support and improve the students rather than lessons having the potential to cause disengagement and to deter learning if the student does not have at least a basic level of understanding.

This therefore means that, where necessary, students should be provided with additional support through small intervention sessions that can be used to build necessary knowledge and understanding. These sessions offer the opportunity to:

- Engage students in one-to-one conversation, either with the teacher or a peer (with a suggested topic) in order to build confidence in communication.

- Provide the opportunity to work collaboratively, engaging in tasks that require a dialogue in order to achieve the objective. This could be done in tasks such as:

    - creating a menu in a restaurant

    - explaining a mathematical equation or a scientific topic

    - obtaining information on a different culture.

- Encourage general communication and conversation in English through the introduction of games that involve communication. Monopoly provides opportunity for interaction, whilst games like Cluedo provide a script that can be followed (there's also the opportunity to use Scrabble for literacy development).

One of the key contributing factors to the success of this strategy is the opportunity for students to engage with and share their own culture with others. It is important that students are given this opportunity to share their culture and that this is actively encouraged instead of integration into mainstream English-speaking academia being the sole focus. This can be achieved by considering the following strategies:

- Allowing the student to share their favourite song, book or film from their first language.

- Possibly encouraging the student to teach a peer (or even the teacher) basic elements of their first language. By using English as the neutral language, students can teach each other basic phrases including:

  - Hello/Goodbye

  - My name is...

  - I am...years old

  - Numbers from 1 to 10.

- Providing them with the opportunity to present a short speech about themselves and where they grew up, and encouraging the students to speak English to a small group of peers in order to develop confidence.

It may not be possible to conduct some of the strategies that have been mentioned above with students who have already been integrated into mainstream education. In these circumstances, it is vital that the classroom practitioner recognise the mammoth task these students are performing on a day-to-day basis. Not only are they developing knowledge and learning in English, they are then translating this into their first language in order to process the information and support retention.

In either approach (intervention or mainstream), there are processes that need to be taken into consideration in planning and preparation to support the learning.

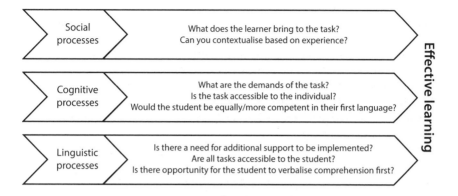

Consideration of these processes immediately provides an opportunity for the practitioner to reflect on whether a learning task is accessible to the student. From this, it is possible to support knowledge and language acquisition by ensuring that education provides the opportunity for students to:

- Collaborate with peers and share their knowledge through active discussion.

- Have access to models that can support them in developing automaticity of required skills.

- Be provided with visual stimuli that can allow students to associate vocabulary with images to support cognitive development. In these circumstances, dual coding is an effective approach alongside the implementation of knowledge organisers that are accessible in all lessons.

- Foster independence and appreciate students' confidence and capabilities. This includes allowing students to write notes, research and revise in their first language.

Approaching EAL and SEND approaches separately should allow practitioners to distinguish between EAL and SEND. At times there can be an unnecessary association between the two, with the misconception that an inability to communicate in a certain language suggests that a student is not able in a subject – a critical misconception that could damage the learning and confidence of that student.

There are, however, circumstances where the two access inhibitors (EAL and SEND) may overlap. A small proportion of EAL students do have additional learning/social/emotional/behavioural needs alongside their linguistic requirements. Determining the difference between EAL and SEND can often be complex and confusing, but this is yet another reason why it is crucial that the correct procedures are put in place in the initial introduction of the student so that these assessments and judgements can be made quickly and the necessary support implemented. Whether dealing with both or just one inhibiting factor, the implementation of the teaching cycle into your everyday practice can support the development of all learners through clear instruction alongside effective communication.

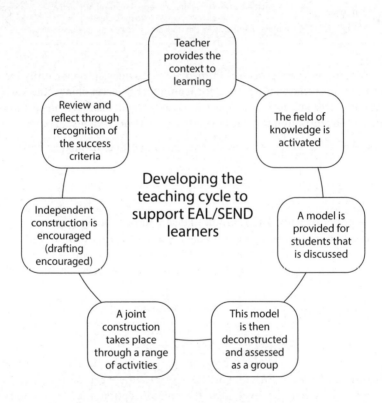

UNDERSTANDING THE KEY TO EFFECTIVE COMMUNICATION

When people talk, listen completely. Most people never listen.

Ernest Hemingway

Not all communication is verbal. Although we need to encourage our students to articulate their ideas, they also need to comprehend that communication is a sum of all its parts. When we communicate, there are a wealth of components that we need to consider. As has already been discussed in the opening chapter, to truly comprehend oracy skills we must revisit the oracy framework in order to ensure that learners can understand and appreciate their recognition of the four key areas:

- linguistic
- physical
- cognitive
- social and emotional.

The physical aspects of oracy are often the most overlooked when we teach oracy in the classroom. Although we discuss verbalisation of ideas and the ability to articulate with a degree of intelligence, the recognition on non-verbal cues, such as body language, is often overlooked.

According to experts, these non-verbal signals make up a huge part of daily communication. If students are introduced to this concept, they should be able to understand that, from our facial expressions to our body movements, the things we *don't* say can still convey volumes of information.

Understanding body language is important, but it is also essential to pay attention to other cues such as context. We need to instil in our learners that the recognition of cues and the ability to read body language is necessary in any form of communication. As practitioners, we are constantly required to shape our dialogue and approach through the recognition of those silent cues that we are offered by the audience. Some of these visual cues include:

- heads on the desk
- messing with a piece of equipment
- wandering eyes or a focus on another object/person in the room
- doodling and drawing unnecessary pictures (although this can often be a technique adopted by higher performers to aid concentration).

Recognising the warning signals that show your students have become disengaged with learning often depends on your ability to understand and contextualise the audience in front of you. It may be that it is the need to remain active that leads someone to mess with something; it could also be that the listener's head is down because they are making notes based on what you're saying. It is the responsibility of the educator to gauge when these signals indicate a juxtaposition to the intention. These issues can easily be counteracted through the incorporation of strategies to promote self-awareness within the students as to what effective communication looks like in most situations. One example is the use of SLANT as a school initiative:

- Sit up: upright but relaxed.
- Listen: thinking about content and clarifying any misconceptions.
- Ask and answer: ensure that you are participating in a dialogue where applicable.
- Never interrupt: listen and indicate when you would like to contribute.
- Track the speaker: where possible, keep your eye on the speaker.

The idea is that, if we explicitly instil in our students what active listening looks like, we are allowing them to develop an automaticity that can support them throughout their career. Although it may not always be the case, this could ultimately prevent any misconception around engagement.

An understanding of the significance of non-verbal cues can then be developed in more depth by allowing students to recognise certain scientifically recognised 'tells' or indicators that could be used to support interactions. There are several components of body language that we can recognise and use to interpret true feelings or emotions in others. These include:

- posture
- gestures

- tone of voice (this will be discussed in more detail later on)
- eye contact
- breathing
- proximity
- facial expressions.

Although we must acknowledge the holistic picture in order to consider the overall message, generally children from a young age are able to gauge facial expressions without any type of explicit teaching. This is because facial expressions are among the most universal forms of body language.

When we consider gestures, messages can very easily be misconstrued depending on factors such as the audience and the corresponding culture. For example, Richard Brooks discussed the idea that certain gestures that we commonly associate with our culture, and may use in day-to-day conversations, can actually be perceived differently in various environments. He explains:

> Consider the 'OK' sign. Seems innocuous enough, unless you're in France or Belgium, when it might mean '0' or 'worthless.' Or in Brazil, Germany, Russia, Tunisia, Greece, the Middle East and parts of South America, where it's a crude insult. In the Arab world, it can also be used as a curse.
>
> And what about the 'thumbs up' sign? It might seem like an easy way to signal approval, but in countries like Australia, New Zealand, Africa, South America, Afghanistan, Iran, and parts of Italy and Greece, you might be unwittingly inviting your conversation partner to 'Sit on it!' How awkward.
>
> Meanwhile, the 'V' for victory sign is another gesture with many meanings, some of them obscene. It could mean 'victory,' it could mean 'peace,' or it could mean 'up yours.'
>
> What about pointing? Not in Malaysia, where [it's] taboo to point with an index finger. Use your thumb instead! Making lots of grand sweeping gestures is almost a necessity in countries like Italy, where people 'talk with their hands.' But in other countries, like Japan, it's considered rude. (Brooks, 2016)

To support this further, there is clear validity in the concept of proximity, which is also reflective of a behaviour management technique that was once taught. The concept of being able to label different zones of proximity was originally described by Edward T. Hall in his 1966 publication *The Hidden Dimension*. In this, he suggested that where you are positioned can have a lot of weighting on the progression and the outcome of a conversation. As a practitioner, the understanding of proximity can also support your ability to communicate with the class and maintain a fixed learning environment.

Handel's proximity zones

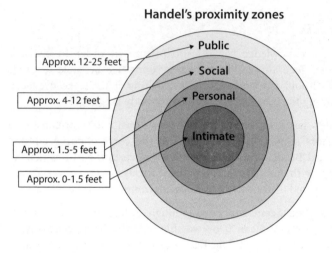

The public zone

A generalised space where interaction is limited. Typically involving a monologic approach, this type of distance is created in assemblies or lecture sessions. In these types of environments, clarity through volume and pitch is particularly significant.

The social zone

A space more suited to the classroom. Within this zone of proximity, it will be easier to move between monologic and dialogic approaches to teaching. You can also encourage more interaction without fear of students feeling uncomfortable or perhaps ostracised.

The personal zone

This can be perceived as the attention 'sweet spot'. In many environments, this is what we might refer to as the 'comfort zone', meaning that it is the distance where communication appears more collaborative and there is likely to be more active listening and attentiveness from the recipient.

By 'working the room' when we speak, and by distributing ourselves in different areas instead of one fixed point, we are able to pass through an individual's personal zone. The concept of us, as class teachers, just being visitors at this level of proximity is helpful in ensuring the attention of students. It could be hypothesised that the sudden spark of attention that students get when you move closer to them is almost like an alarm going off, indicating that this zone has been breached. Their reaction is almost instinctual.

However, if we need to have a discussion with a student, the idea that we are then in this zone for a longer period of time needs to be taken into consideration. What could be used as a strategy of engagement and attention all of a sudden could become uncomfortable and confrontational.

From a teacher–student perspective, longer periods of time should only be spent within this zone if a dialogue is taking place. It is often acknowledged that we can utilise these zones as a behaviour management strategy to gain the attention of an individual whose behaviour is deviating from expectations. Just be aware that the longer you are in this area, the more you may find that the student's intimate circle is expanding.

From a peer-to-peer perspective, a joint understanding about how to communicate in these circumstances is easily reciprocated. Close proximity allows students to feel comfortable when collaborating and discussing without the students becoming unsettled or apprehensive.

The intimate zone

This is the area in which we can find the most problems. In our day-to-day lives, consider the times when individuals invade our intimate space. Whether it be on public transport or when moving through a crowded corridor, it is quite common to feel that surge of claustrophobia creeping up on you. If we can relate the trigger for someone entering our intimate zone to an alarm, this breach is a siren!

The result of this proximity from a teacher–student point of view is more than likely going to be confrontation or some form of channelled aggression. Most of us react in the same way in situations where we feel this area is being invaded, so no one ought to be surprised if the attempt to use this as a behaviour management strategy goes wrong.

Interestingly, if we consider seating allocations in a classroom environment, where there are two students to a table, then students are, in essence, in each other's intimate zone. No matter what your perspective on the groupings versus rows debate that appears to be a thorn in the side of most practitioners, the current conditions within the education system are actually endorsing classrooms of a larger size. However, with a substantial lack of space or equipment, there is a high concentration of students who are sharing their intimate zone with others.

Unfortunately, there is no clear-cut suggestion as to how to resolve this issue, except for advocating for small class sizes and more space, both of which I'm afraid are out of our grasp in most schools across the country at the moment.

Reading body language

> Nature has given us two ears, two eyes, and but one tongue – to the end that we should hear and see more than we speak.
>
> **Socrates**

The facial expressions used to convey fear, anger, sadness and happiness are similar throughout the world. Micro-expressions are a type of facial expression that happen unconsciously and last only between 1/25 to 1/15 of a second. They happen extremely fast, but, if you learn to catch them, they can reveal a lot about what a person is thinking or feeling – even when they are trying to hide something. These are the techniques that are used by gamblers during poker games, or by law enforcement during interrogations.

Consider when you ask students in your class if they understand something. As practitioners, we are trained to incorporate formative assessment strategies in these moments to gain a quantifiable summary of the current learning environment. However, this approach is only half of the assessment. We intuitively recognise that actions speak louder than words; therefore, what is perceived and what is real can be substantially different. More often than not, students' demeanour and the signals that they subconsciously present are actually more trustworthy than their verbal or conscious responses.

Recognition of these signals provides an immediate impression of the true thoughts and feelings of your respondent. Research even suggests that we make judgements about people's intelligence based upon their faces and expressions. Paul Ekman has found support for the universality of a variety of facial expressions tied to particular emotions including joy, fear, anger, surprise and sadness. Not only can the ability to read these signs be vital for practitioners in reading into student perception and comprehension more accurately, but the explicit teaching of these signs could also serve to develop the social and emotional capabilities of learners. The ability of students to read signs and cues could ultimately prevent bullying or many kinds of uncomfortable conversations.

The arms and legs can also be useful in conveying non-verbal information. Crossing the arms can indicate defensiveness. Crossing legs away from another person may indicate dislike or discomfort with that individual. Other subtle signals such as expanding the arms widely may be an attempt to seem larger or more commanding, while keeping the arms close to the body may be an effort to minimise oneself or withdraw oneself from the attention of another/others.

When you are evaluating body language, pay attention to some of the following signals that the arms and legs may convey:

- **Standing with hands placed on the hips** can be an indication that a person is ready and in control, or it can also be a sign of aggressiveness.
- **Clasping the hands behind the back** might indicate that a person is feeling bored, anxious, or even angry.
- **Rapidly tapping fingers or fidgeting** can be a sign that a person is bored, impatient, or frustrated.
- **Crossed legs** can indicate that a person is feeling closed off or in need of privacy.

Wang (2009) hypothesised the following meanings behind particular examples of body language:

- **Crossed arms:** A closed-off posture implies resistance. 'People might just be cold, but the stereotype is that they aren't listening', according to Ronald Riggio, director of the Kravis Leadership Institute at Claremont McKenna College.
- **A brief touch to the hand:** This captures your attention and forms a quick connection. But towards students or peers, make sure the action doesn't appear condescending or predatory. This can also interfere with the recipient's intimate space within their zone of proximity, which needs to be carefully considered.
- **A nose rub:** This motion is often linked with deception. If you notice people doing this while you talk, you could be coming across as disingenuous.
- **A barrier:** Personal space is sacred for most people, with the majority of us having a clear understanding of just how close is too close. There may, however, be some people who do not recognise the importance of this personal space. As a subconscious reaction, you may find either yourself or your learner creating a barrier of some form between them and you. It may not be explicit, but this is a clear indication that the occupant has a comfort zone that is currently being breached.
- **A hand placed under the chin:** Generally, when you see this gesture, a decision is being made. This action could also suggest a captivated audience leaning in to engage with the dialogue further.
- **Feet pointed toward the door:** Some say the feet are the most honest part of the body, so no matter how mesmerised people seem to be,

this may prove they're actually over it. When asking students to stay behind if you need to talk to them, it might be beneficial to sit them back down facing away from the door. This way, the entire body is focussed on a fixed point that is not associated with departure or exit.

- **A back-of-the-neck scratch:** Your student might have an itch, but it could mean they still have questions and/or concerns.

Drama can be used to incorporate these ideas into your lesson, in particular focussing specifically on the acting used to depict thoughts and emotions.

Subject-specific example (English):

In JB Priestley's *An Inspector Calls*, Act three (the final act) focusses the audience's attention on the grievous misgivings of Eric Birling and his atrocious contribution to the eventual suicide of Eva Smith. In this act, we (as the audience) are able to connect the dots and develop a sense of dramatic irony as we solve the puzzle of his participation before the rest of the characters do. All of a sudden, the play provides a domino effect showing the actors' realisation of what has happened and this is communicated through actions as opposed to through vocalisation specifically.

In the 2019 BBC rendition of the play, in which the actors were able to exhibit extensive cues through their body language, students were provided with the following task:

Watch the video in the link from 56:00 minutes. This is the moment where we find out Eric's horrible secret.

In your books, record the key visual cues that each of the characters display. Once you have watched it, answer the following questions:

1. *Who is the first to realise Eric is the father?*
2. *Does Mr Birling know the truth?*
3. *What is the significance of the inspector rising?*
4. *Does Gerald know?*
5. *How does Mrs Birling's presentation change?*

Having been provided with this task, the students were consequently able to gain a deeper understanding of the significance of stage directions and how these should be interpreted. Although this is a very subject-specific example, the task can be used as a catalyst to consider the effectiveness of visual cues in day-to-day life.

Incorporating body language in the classroom

In the same way that we need to explicitly and implicitly teach oracy skills in the classroom in order to support our students' development, we must also consider how we go on to model these skills and techniques in our own manner. Teachers or lecturers have an important role in recognising and practising effective communication skills. It may be daunting, but our actions and words are under scrutiny and absorbed on a constant basis. This means that not only should we consider our awareness of the actions of our students, but we also need to reflect on how we can utilise strategies to develop our own skills.

When we think about how we teach, it is important to recognise from a leadership perspective that we (in a similar manner to our students) are all unique individuals. We all have a particular dialect, stance and walk. Through effective coaching, we need to embrace and develop our foundations to support each individual style instead of perceiving a set strategy and formula that should be embedded by all.

All staff are professionals. Adherence to school policies whilst having high expectations of all learners can easily be achieved in numerous environments and through numerous strategies. Consider the difference between a PE lesson and a maths lesson, or even a drama lesson as opposed to an English lesson. The ability to manage a class and ensure that learning is taking place is not fundamentally confined to a specific style of teaching. Instead, it requires an ability to adapt, reflect and manage that will provide the steps to success.

With this in mind, there are still more ways in which we incorporate body language into our lessons that can be utilised by most (if not all) practitioners:

- **Anchoring**

  The concept of anchoring is one that we may already use subconsciously without even recognising it as a strategy. According to some:

  Anchoring is a neuro linguistic programming (NLP) technique rooted in the Pavlovian conditioning tradition where a stimulus can evoke a specific response. Scientists have concluded that if we keep pairing two things together, the brain begins to see them as one. The key here is repetition: Repeat the pairing often enough and soon, one will trigger the other. (Stevie, 2020)

  Anchoring your lessons allows students to retain information in their long-term memory through association. This can be used in any subject setting, but it is particularly useful when you consider subjects such as modern foreign languages. This is where we begin to see a more generalised interpretation of actions related to sounds.

The most common way to recognise this concept is to consider how we ourselves have anchored particular words to particular actions. Imagine that you are in a crowded room and you can't hear anyone. Think about what signs you might use to:

- ask for the bill
- explain that you are unsure
- request a drink
- tell someone that you are okay or fine.

Take, for example, a Spanish lesson in which you are teaching students that the word for love is 'amor'. You may choose to connect this symbol to the formation of both hands into a love heart (or whatever gesture you choose). The constant repetition of this word alongside this action enables students to recognise the embedded associations. In essence, it's like dual coding but using your body instead of with symbols!

- **Exaggeration**

As Shakespeare once said, 'all the world's a stage and all the men and women are merely players'. No matter how much you believe that your teaching style is completely natural and authentic, there will always be some element of acting required. There will always be instances where your own personal feelings are not those to be transmitted in a classroom. We're all human, and it's important to recognise this fact. There will be days where we may be under the weather, stressed, tired or restless. What is important is that this does not affect the way we present information.

The concept of exaggeration is often relevant when teaching larger groups (even assemblies or lectures that include a large number of participants in a traditionally monologic situation), and is often associated with theatre acting. The ability to make actions bigger and voices louder without coming across as shouting or particularly flamboyant is an important skill. This can also be true of facial expressions, although we must consider authenticity and the risk of students questioning our mental state if we begin flapping around the classroom and becoming overly emotional at the death of Mercutio.

Students need to be enthused and inspired, but they should not feel like they are being conned by a human teacher. It's about finding a realistic middle ground between an automaton and a theatrical performer.

Exaggeration is about bringing an element of grandeur to your statements. The technique involves avoiding a disregard of any form of gesture and even of gesturing timidly. Instead, the action should contain an element of hyperbole. Exaggeration as a memory technique to support recall is a helpful tool, but one that also needs to be contextualised and adapted to your own style and approach. Always remember that there is a fine line between accentuated body language and over-the-top acting.

- **Voice Modulation**

The concept of voice modulation brings with it an endless debate on appropriate volume for projection in the classroom. Voice modulation isn't necessarily about causing a booming sound to echo across the classroom, stopping everyone in their tracks. It's the ability to gain attention using methods that can be classed as less invasive or aggressive.

Sound is often a key tool to gain the attention of your learner. Whether noises are subtle or louder and more obvious signs of attention-seeking, the aim is typically to gain the attention of those in the near vicinity. In a later chapter, we will consider the concept of tone in more detail, but the significance of volume also plays a large part in the perception of what is being spoken and how it is presented to the audience.

The idea of being able to monitor and control the volume in a classroom is often misconstrued; it is often misinterpreted as endorsing silence amongst learners and the necessity for communication to be kept to a minimum. This is where teachers often become apprehensive about embedding oracy skills into their classroom.

Students need to be aware of is how they can control their volume effectively through performing situational analysis and considering their audience so that they can alter their volume accordingly. Whilst it is important for the teacher to modulate their own voice in order to come across in a positive manner, the same needs to be considered for our students.

The Eyes

The eyes are frequently referred to as the 'windows to the soul', since they are capable of revealing a great deal about what a person is feeling or thinking. When evaluating body language, students and practitioners alike should pay attention to the following eye signals:

Eye Gaze – When a person looks directly into your eyes while having a conversation, it indicates that they are interested and paying attention. However, prolonged eye contact can feel threatening.

Blinking – Blinking is natural, but you should also pay attention to whether a person is blinking too much or too little. People often blink more rapidly when they are feeling distressed or uncomfortable. Infrequent blinking may indicate that a person is intentionally trying to control his or her eye movements.

Pupil Size – Pupil size can be a very subtle nonverbal communication signal. While light levels in the environment control pupil dilation, sometimes emotions can also cause small changes in pupil size.

Eye contact is the main way we determine if a person is paying attention to us and actually engaged in social interaction. Although we need to recognise that some individuals may intrinsically have a problem with maintaining eye contact, for the majority, eye contact is a clear indication of whether or not you have a learner's focus. This is the reason why the use of visual recognition from students has also been integrated into the SLANT approach.

In a generalised interpretation, when individuals make eye contact with us while speaking, we tend to find that they exhibit evidence of a more positive communication experience. We generally associate these conversations as including confidence, clarity and the presentation of a more personalised approach. When individuals make eye contact while listening to us, we know that they are actually paying attention to us and absorbing what we are saying.

Meanwhile, in some circumstances, lack of eye contact can come off as evidence of boredom, shyness, upset or deception. It can also be a sign of depression and mental health problems. When we fail at making healthy eye contact with others, it hurts our ability to connect with people in the best way possible. It could be perceived that people either don't trust us or that they think we don't like them.

Noah Zandan accentuates the necessity of eye contact by relating our usage to a biological evolution. He states:

> As background, we know that because of evolution it is easy for humans to 'speak' with their eyes. An article from the *New York Times* points

out 'neither chimpanzees nor any of the other 220 species of nonhuman primates have whites of the eyes.' Anthropologists believe that we developed a white backdrop for the iris and pupils of our eyes so that others can easily tell where we are looking. It is believed this serves the purpose of cooperation – we are able to cooperate faster and easier with each other through the use of our eyes. (Zandan, 2020)

He then goes on to reiterate the significance of eye contact by referencing the statistical analysis collated by a communications analytics database:

Adults make eye contact between 30% and 60% of the time in an average conversation. However, to make an emotional connection, the ideal amount of eye contact is between 60% and 70%. We also found that direct eye contact that is held for more than 10 seconds at a time is unnerving for the person you are talking to. As opportunities for face-to-face interactions in the workplace decline, it is important to take advantage of their benefits when they do occur, through effective eye-contact. (Zandan, 2020)

As previously explained, the effectiveness of eye contact should still be moderated and carefully thought about. There needs to be a balance that is maintained throughout a conversation so that there is less risk of someone coming across as either intense or superficial. It is appropriate to take breaks and look away from time to time, and it's natural for our eyes to move around while we talk to others.

Eye contact can also play a part in effective behaviour management. Sometimes, maintaining a conversation with the whole class and at the same time making eye contact with a student who seems to be disengaged from learning may be enough to act as a warning to that student. By acknowledging that what they are doing is not acceptable, but without shifting the dialogue or changing focus, a teacher can show that they have recognised the negative behaviour without advertising it.

The same strategy can be used with body language. By maintaining the dialogue and shifting your body so that you accentuate the fact that your main focus is on the rest of the class, you can acknowledge the behaviour of a student with just a hand signal. This can diminish the recognition the student receives for their actions. By eliminating the significance of their actions, you prevent any unnecessary attention serving as a reward for deviant behaviour.

Like all non-verbal communication, eye contact can reveal a lot about our thoughts and feelings. When someone looks away after we ask them a question, it could mean they are trying to hide something. Or when someone looks us straight in the eye while answering a question, it usually means they are being very honest and straightforward – though they may be trying hard to lie convincingly!

Improving your ability to make eye contact

For some, the idea of making eye contact can be daunting and intimidating, and confidence is an important consideration. Imagine the student, whom most teachers will encounter at some stage of their career, for whom conversation and dialogue appears to come far too easily. They are the student whom you feel you spend more time encouraging to demonstrate other skills aside from their ability to verbalise. Now consider the change in the body language and eye contact of this student when you ask them to read out something they wrote, or you ask them a question that requires them to develop a deeper understanding. This student may demonstrate a distinct shift in their ability to maintain eye contact. They may utilise their paper as a barrier (or a shield) behind which they do not have to maintain any eye contact.

By asking them to expose their intellect and comprehension, the effectiveness of their presentation depends directly on their confidence in their own knowledge acquisition and skills. This is similar to encouraging speeches or debates (both of which will be explored in more detail later).

One of the best ways to improve your eye contact with others is to practise the 'triangle method'.

Ask students to focus their attention on their partner following a triangle structure. By asking them to shift their focus from one eye to the other eye and then to the person's lips, you are taking the first steps towards making eye contact seem less uncomfortable.

This creates an invisible 'triangle shape' on the person's face.

If you feel like your students are not quite ready for using this technique with their partners, you could start by using images to get them used to the concept. Ask them to hold their gaze on each of the three sections by focussing on the first eye (1), holding it for a couple seconds, moving to the next eye (2), holding it for a couple seconds, moving to the lips (3), holding it for a couple seconds, then moving back to the first eye (1) and holding it for another couple of seconds.

This could then be turned into a game in which you could ask questions that incorporate the students' ability to demonstrate eye contact alongside their ability to recognise particular facial expressions, such as:

- What colour was the person's eyes?
- What emotion could you suggest this person is exhibiting? Why?

Eye contact is a tremendously important aspect of all communication – and it's important to identify to students how and why this skill can be utilised in all elements of their post-academic careers. Whether it is about building trust or exhibiting confidence, effective eye contact is the catalyst to efficiency in oracy.

The mouth

Mouth expressions and movements can also be essential in reading body language. For example, chewing on the bottom lip may indicate that the individual is experiencing feelings of worry, fear or insecurity.

Covering the mouth may be an effort to be polite if the person is yawning or coughing, but it may also be an attempt to cover up a frown of disapproval.

Smiling is perhaps one of the greatest body language signals, but smiles can also be interpreted in many ways. A smile may be genuine, or it may be used to express false happiness, sarcasm or even cynicism.

When evaluating body language, pay attention to the following mouth and lip signals:

- **Pursed lips** – Tightening the lips might be an indicator of distaste, disapproval or distrust.

- **Lip biting** – People sometimes bite their lips when they are worried, anxious or stressed.

- **Covering the mouth** – When people want to hide an emotional reaction, they might cover their mouth in order to avoid displaying smiles or smirks.

CASE STUDY 2 – ORACY IN KEY STAGE 5 SCIENCE

Robert Murray-Green has taught A level chemistry for twelve years at two 'outstanding' sixth form colleges. He has been a curriculum leader in chemistry for the last nine years, and has managed teaching both AQA and OCR A level chemistry specifications. Under his supervision, Robert's classes have a robust track record of achievement above all national averages. He also has a strong online e-learning presence with a well-established YouTube channel of short tutorials. As a result of this, he was nominated for an 'innovative teaching award' in 2018.

In post-16 study of science, most of a learner's oracy is focussed on the development of accuracy and precision with scientific vocabulary. Topics covered are often an extension of content covered already at GCSE. In order to make progress with the increasing level of detail, an expansion of the learner's vocabulary is necessary to efficiently communicate new processes and old ones more efficiently. Subjects such as chemistry and physics at A level also start to resemble their position as 'physical sciences' and, in doing so, place more of their focus on mathematical skills and short written analysis but using enhanced vocabulary.

The emphasis on the source of the new vocabulary also differs a lot between the sciences. In biology for instance, new vocabulary is often used to name components of cells that have not been studied before by learners at GCSE. The new names for the cell organelles (for example) and then their roles in processes is a big challenge. Learners have to work quite hard to not only recall and suitably name the newly encountered cell components, but also then describe their role in the cell. For example, most GCSE learners are familiar with DNA replication taking place in the nucleus of the cell. At A level, however, learners must incorporate new, smaller cell organelles (such as ribosomes) and enhanced detail in the process/aspects of DNA replication (such as bases and codons).

In chemistry, GCSE learners will study the details of alkene molecules and their reactions. Transitioning to A level, learners then need to incorporate the terms sigma, pi and orbital to describe their structure and explain concepts such as electrophilic addition to describe their reactions. It is a very stark and sudden increase in demand. Making this a part of their everyday vocabulary in class is a challenging but essential part of their development. Activities, such as those which challenge learners to describe processes but without the use of their new vocabulary, draw attention to the new demand and necessity of the new material. A temporary 'banned word list' of all the new terms in an 'articulate' style game format is a creative way to form/update a vocabulary list.

Other challenges surround the presence of terms that have dual meanings both within and outside science. To most people, the term 'organic', for instance, would refer to the method of farming used to grow/raise different types of food they can buy in a supermarket. To an A level chemistry student, however, it refers to structures that contain carbon atoms. Outside of the classroom, it is then quite challenging to provide spoken examples of how to accurately use such terms in a scientific context. Much of the material available to the wider public does not carry the level of detail required for post-16 learners. Most podcasts and TV media are aimed at a GCSE level and non-scientific audiences.

As a result of this, confidence with naming items that have never been encountered before is a challenge. Often students remain silent for fear of mispronunciation. To try to prevent this, words are often introduced prior to their actual context and the origin of components of the word are discussed to allow them to provide suggestion for the possible appropriate context. In chemistry, for example, the term 'mondentate' is introduced to students during their second year of study. By breaking the word down to its components of 'mono' (one) and 'dentate' (tooth-like), students can better visualise the model to which the word applies. When they do begin to practise this vocabulary, students often 'throw around' terms in the early stages when describing concepts and see what sticks in terms of accuracy. This can lead to long-term misconceptions and very often contradictions if not challenged.

A major part of post-16 education is the short 2-year window before final examinations. Short sentences, scientific vocabulary, precise terms and concise responses are praised. In post-16 science, often bullet points are encouraged in written work, which then is translated into class responses. Subjects at post-16 differ widely in the writing style that learners need to develop. Often, the impression that learners should do a range of subjects to 'keep their options open' is celebrated by establishments. Actually, in doing so, the learner can end up in very contrasting environments when it comes to assessment style.

To summarise the key factors and approaches to consider when adopting post-16 oracy strategies from a science point of view:

- Fine-tuning vocabulary exposure and comprehension is now even more significant, and it needs to be streamlined for use in an exam.

- Often, mid-grade students get described as 'great in class but weaker on paper', as they are able to perhaps say more and engage with the terms when they speak to others, while on paper they struggle to exhibit the same strength. This could be associated with the limitless space they have to discuss a concept compared to the very limited space they have to write a response to an exam question. Perhaps they are not challenged enough with word count when they speak?

- Significant subject clash – e.g. history vs chemistry. The assessment style of subjects can vary widely and student who have had poor advice and guidance on selecting their A levels can struggle if not self-aware.

- There can be more pressure to make rapid progress, as the 16–18 window is narrow even before exams start.

- Students given mock interviews (for university) often perform well based on feedback, but visibly struggle with initially verbalising topics that they could easily score 10/10 with in a written assessment. The more practise and exposure that students can be provided with, the more confident and articulate their responses.

- In subjects like science, there are few role models of correct and accessible use of spoken scientific language. Commonly, wider media simplifies terms to suit a non-scientific audience. When looking at how to support this, podcasting could be an avenue to introduce to those students wanting to gain further information.

RECOGNISING YOUR VOICE

Alongside body language, the ability to interpret voice is also significant for the physical elements of the oracy skills framework. The perception of the voice and its significance can be determined by several intrinsic factors:

- the projection of your own voice as the facilitator
- the tone of voice and recognising variations and their effect on interpretation
- the pace of speaking and how this contributes to interpretation.

The easiest way to accentuate the necessity of voice appreciation is to consider the implications of when the voice is incoherent or even dysphonic. In their research into the impact of the teacher's voice in the classroom, Rodrigues et al. state that:

The teacher, being a facilitator in the teaching-learning dynamic, plays the key role of eliciting changes in the students through the use of voice. (2017)

They also allude to the idea that:

The classroom is a dynamic space of communication where language and the teacher's expressive resources promote social interactions. The type of voice of the teacher, in this setting, can be a motivating or discouraging factor for students.

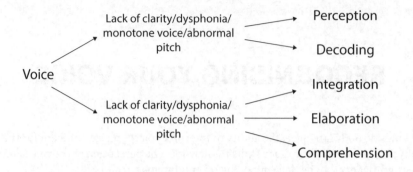

Put simply, the voice from which the information is emitted has a substantial effect on the comprehension and retention of information. If the voice of the facilitator demonstrates a lack of clarity, a monotonal pitch, an overtly low or high volume or even dysphonia, then most of the cognitive process is allocated to perception or decoding the information. On the other hand, if the learning is relayed in a clear, well-articulated manner, integration, elaboration and comprehension can occur.

The projection of your own voice as the facilitator

The term 'dysphonic' refers to a voice that can be classified as 'abnormal' – hoarse, rough or raspy. According to Martins et al. (2014), the prevalence of dysphonia in teachers accounts for up to 80% of the cohort. Martins et al. emphasise that the effect is multidimensional and can have a significantly negative impact on the quality of life of those teachers. Developing a raspy and strained sound in our voices is ultimately inevitable if we do not heed the warning signs. When we consider the parameters of our occupation, the strain that is put on our vocal cords on a day-to-day basis is comparable to none except perhaps that put on the voice of a seasoned stage actor.

Rodrigues et al. (2016) identified the implications not only on the profession, but also on the learning of students. They concluded that there are a variety of contributing factors that impede learning, but that the controllable issues include:

- **The environment** – According to the study, a noisy classroom can have a detrimental effect on knowledge acquisition in certain circumstances. This reiterated the need for adaptive teaching. Incorporating dialogic teaching strategies does not necessarily impede the learning, but can be used to develop the understanding once it is provisionally introduced. This is reflective of how universities provide lectures that are then followed by seminars.

Speech Rate – In 1998, Schmidt (referenced by Rodrigues et al.) suggested that speech rate is an effective strategy that is commonly utilised by expressive teachers. The ability to incorporate strategic pauses into dialogue, alongside the ability to adapt articulation and pitch depending on sex and age, is important for learning.

Student evaluation of voice – Not only does student evaluation impact on knowledge retention, but it also impacts on the attention and focus of the learner. Intrinsically, the more resources that are being utilised by the recipient to gather the information, the less capacity there is available to store what is being presented.

Tips for teachers

When you are teaching:

- Ensure that you are showing an awareness of the surroundings; your volume in a classroom will be substantially lower than your volume in a hall or outside. Recognising your environment and adjusting you pitch and tone accordingly can help to support comprehension and also perception. If a teacher comes across as shouting and screaming, this can often be recognised as a sign of loss of control. There may be those who disagree, but when you consider instances where you might find yourself shouting in day-to-day life, you can see there is a clear correlation between the two.

- When we become stressed, we can sometimes alter the pitch of our voice and present a higher, less comfortable tone for recipients. This can be resolved through an awareness of the difference between speaking from your chest and speaking through your throat. It is common knowledge that teachers are prone to sore throats and, more often than not, this can be rectified through the recognition and correct use of breathing muscles. A quick tip to distinguish between the two would be to hum. If you can feel your lips vibrating, this is an indicator that you are breathing and controlling the sound from your diaphragm; if your lips don't vibrate, this is because you are breathing from your throat and are therefore more likely to cause strain through constant use.

The tone of voice and recognising the variations and their effect on interpretations

Tone of voice is an integral component that needs to be explicitly taught to students in both their academic studies and from a pastoral perspective. When we consider the implications of the incorrect tone in certain circumstances, we are once again preparing our students for situations that they will face post-academia. In subject-specific circumstances, the implications of how tone can affect inference is commonly delivered through English and drama.

The ability to distinguish between positive and negative tones through specific examples is beneficial not only to comprehend others, but also to support self-awareness and the presentation of oneself to others.

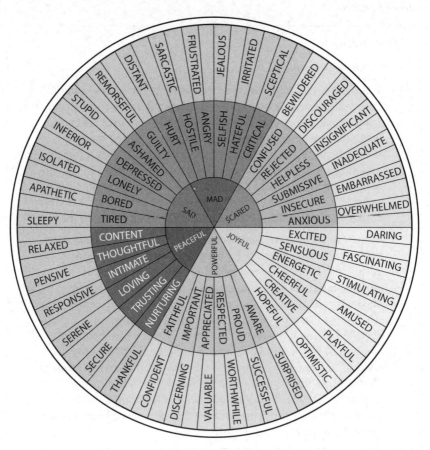

The ability for students to recognise variations in tone will provide them with an awareness of audience-specific communication strategies.

It has been implied that certain styles of voices are perceived negatively by listeners. In 2015, Brännström et al. stated that 'such voices tend to be monotonous and to show limited pitch variation, which may make is harder for students to sustain their attention in the message transmitted by the teacher' (Brännström et al., 2015).

The pace of speaking and how this contributes to interpretations

As practitioners, our ITT (initial teacher training) year appeared to be consumed by the concept of pace. Lesson plans were intrinsically mapped out to within seconds, and the concept of allowing the lesson to lead itself based on learner comprehension was practically frowned upon. The fact of the matter is that if pace is too slow, learners may stop paying attention, or the momentum may lead to deviation from behaviour expectations. Alternatively, a quickened pace may result in a lack of comprehension. The concept of pace hampering language processing is a factor that needs to be considered when we are approaching the planning and presentation of information.

In certain circumstances, a quick and energetic pace is beneficial so that students remain on task and focussed on the learning process. In other circumstances, the pace may need to be slower to ensure that all students comprehend the objectives. Whether adopting a specific lesson structure approach (a rigorous accelerated learning cycle that focusses specifically on a lesson-by-lesson basis) or a less regimental approach, planning is still integral to ensuring that the pace of the lesson is suited to the needs and requirements of all.

In any approach, there are certain considerations that you can adopt:

- Ensure that you are fully aware of the long-term plans of your curriculum, as well as your short-term goals and objectives.
- When moving at a quicker pace, ensure that you are considering how you can incorporate retrieval practise in order to register comprehension.
- A quick pace requires constant use of formative assessment and questioning techniques in order to remain quick as opposed to rushed. In these circumstances, methods that can be used include:
  - (a) Thumbs up or down

- (b) 1–5 scale using hands
- (c) RAG rating.

- Make sure that resources and required additional information are readily to hand. This will allow you to continue to pace without there being a distinct pause.

CASE STUDY 3 – ORACY IN GEOGRAPHY

Jennifer Monk is currently head of geography at Golborne High School. She is a specialist leader of education (SLE) and is also a consultant to the Geographical Association. Jennifer has won an award from the Royal Geographical Society for her excellence in teaching secondary geography.

We use 'speak like a geographer' in a variety of ways in order to support the oracy development of our students. The approach can be used:

- with the grid on the board
- with students each being provided with their own individual copies so that they can have access to the vocabulary
- with students also being encouraged to write down 'excellent words' whilst others are speaking, which they are then encouraged to refer back to and reference.

If you can Speak like a Geographer... Speak

'Ageing populations create benefits and challenges for countries such as the UK.' To what extent do you agree with this statement?

Verbally tell the person sitting next to you your answer to this question. They will give you points for everyword you use accurately. They will subtract points for words in the banned word column.

1 point	2 points	3 points	4 points	−1 point
Pensions	Grey vote	Social	Japan	Like
Taxes	Healthcare/NHS	Economic	Retirement age	Erm
Illness	Birth rate	Life expectancy	Grey pound	I think
Education	Care home	Dependence	Population structure	

 You can write like a Geographer...

I have found that this strategy does work well, as I find my students are quite competitive and they also like being given a blank grid which they can populate. We have some laminated grids that work like a mini whiteboard, which I have found useful too.

If one were to consider how this strategy could possibly be used ineffectively, I think the issue happens if students are trying to use the word in the 'wrong way' just to get points. It is therefore beneficial to always question whether students know the meaning of the more complex words on the grid and possibly even address any potential misconceptions before they arrive.

Along with this approach, students have a 'geographical language' list at the back of their books and they highlight in their writing when they have used these words. I have seen a huge difference in oracy since we introduced these sheets: because of the highlighting, students constantly look back and reflect on the language and use it more frequently when they speak.

SPOKEN LANGUAGE IN THE NATIONAL CURRICULUM

Spoken language in key stages 1 and 2

One of the main reasons for embarking on this journey of discovery was to improve the life skills of our students. The idea that we could work together as a collective group of professionals to enthuse and encourage the confidence and articulation of the next generation was a big incentive.

The issue then appeared to lie in the hands of the National Curriculum and its expectations regarding which subjects should focus on which skills. The recognition across the key skills for spoken language is there, but the vague reference, alongside the fact that the information can be found in the English subject section, presents a crystal clear misconception: oracy skills are only needed in English.

Obviously, this is ludicrous, but it does help to recognise what the DfE classes as its statutory requirements. In the 2014 outline, the documentation specifies that, up until the students leave primary in year 6, all should be taught to:

- listen and respond appropriately to adults and their peers
- ask relevant questions to extend their understanding and knowledge
- use relevant strategies to build their vocabulary
- articulate and justify answers, arguments and opinions
- give well-structured descriptions, explanations and narratives for different purposes, including for expressing feelings
- maintain attention and participate actively in collaborative conversations, staying on topic and initiating and responding to comments
- use spoken language to develop understanding through speculating, hypothesising, imagining and exploring ideas

- speak audibly and fluently with an increasing command of Standard English
- participate in discussions, presentations, performances, role play, improvisations and debates
- gain, maintain and monitor the interest of the listener(s)
- consider and evaluate different viewpoints, attending to and building on the contributions of others
- select and use appropriate registers for effective communication.

(DfE, 2014, p. 18)

Although these statements apply to all years, the content should be taught at a level appropriate to the age of the students. The non-statutory guidelines point out that these skills need to be built on the preceding years, with student competence being developed in spoken language so that students are able to communicate confidently to a range of audiences in a range of contexts. The documentation then goes on to specify that:

> Attention should also be paid to increasing pupils' vocabulary, ranging from describing their immediate world and feelings to developing a broader, deeper and richer vocabulary to discuss abstract concepts and a wider range of topics, and to enhancing their knowledge about language as a whole. Pupils should receive constructive feedback on their spoken language and listening, not only to improve their knowledge and skills but also to establish secure foundations for effective spoken language in their studies at primary school, helping them to achieve in secondary education and beyond. (DfE, 2014)

Once these skills are developed and embedded in key stage 2, the responsibility is then passed to the secondary school to keep encouraging confidence in spoken language skills. Once again, however, the specifics of what is required and expected can be found in the English subject-specific section, through which the focus is placed on students being encouraged to explore the whole curriculum cognitively, socially and linguistically. It is acknowledged that 'spoken language continues to underpin the development of pupils' reading and writing during key stages 3 and 4 and teachers should therefore ensure pupils' confidence and competence in this area continue to develop.' However, there is no reference to this methodology and pedagogical enhancement in any other subject in such rigour.

Spoken language in key stage 4

The implementation of a recorded speaking and listening assessment since the regeneration of the English Language and Literature assessments in 2016 has brought with it an air of controversy as to how English teachers perceive spoken language in an environment that has been plagued by academic rigour and examination-based assessment. In 2014, the DfE specified that:

> Pupils should be taught to speak clearly and convey ideas confidently using Standard English. They should learn to justify ideas with reasons; ask questions to check understanding; develop vocabulary and build knowledge; negotiate; evaluate and build on the ideas of others; and select the appropriate register for effective communication. They should be taught to give well-structured descriptions and explanations and develop their understanding through speculating, hypothesising and exploring ideas. This will enable them to clarify their thinking as well as organise their ideas for writing. (DfE, 2014)

If we broaden our field of understanding further, the Welsh board have also provided a language competency framework that can be used for the assessment of oracy:

Language Competency Framework (Welsh)

	PRE-ENTRY	A1 - ENTRY	A2 - FOUNDATION	B1 - INTERMEDIARY	B2 - HIGHER	C1 - PROFICIENCY
Oral	Able to pronounce the alphabet and say simple words fairly correctly in the school context. Able to introduce themselves and start interacting socially by using familiar everyday phrases, e.g. greetings, thanks, praising a learner and giving simple commands.	Able to introduce themselves and others verbally, able to ask and answer questions on simple information, e.g. relevant to the school context, e.g. where someone lives, what they like to do. Able to use tense and numerals.	Able to contribute to a simple conversation using a range of simple sentences relating to situations relevant to the school context, e.g. everyday themes and different verb tenses.	Able to hold and contribute to a conversation or familiar subjects relating to school and everyday life using a range of simple and complex sentences. Able to describe straightforward – though explanations for their opinion. Beginning to recognise common errors.	Able to communicate using a range of syntax showing an increasing level of accuracy. Able to discuss unfamiliar subjects and specialist subjects. Able to express and justify an opinion. Able to recognise some errors and correct them.	Able to speak extensively on complex matters, present arguments using the correct register. Interacting and leading discussions and extended teaching sessions correctly in the main. Able to self-correct where necessary.

In most Welsh schools, all staff are responsible for including the Welsh Language Competency levels in IDPs (Individual Development Plans).

When we reconsider the English specifications, the examination revamp indicates that, despite the spoken language component being a mandatory element of the English Language assessment, the results will not be counted towards the GCSE grading. This has therefore provided an element of frustration for teachers already consumed by the intricacies of promoting subject knowledge whilst ensuring examination capability. The prospect of having to record and assess the entire year group can have a justifiably negative perception among those who have to conduct these assessments.

However, it is important for all teachers to consider and incorporate the assessment criteria for spoken language into their own lessons. Separated into the classifications of either a pass, merit or distinction, the incorporation of these criteria into a whole-school approach could provide a wealth of positive strategies to promote oracy and develop communication skills.

The Spoken Language success criteria (AQA version, 2015)

Pass Criteria
Is audible
Uses spoken standard English
Expresses straightforward information/ideas/feelings
Makes an attempt to organise and structure his or her presentation
Makes an attempt to meet the needs of the audience
Listen to questions/feedback and provides an appropriate response in a straightforward manner
Merit Criteria
Is audible
Uses spoken standard English
Expresses challenging ideas/information/feelings using a range of vocabulary
Organises and structures his or her presentation clearly and appropriately to meet the needs of the audience
Achieves the purpose of his or her presentation
Listens to questions/feedback, responding formally and in some detail

Distinction criteria
Is audible
Uses spoken standard English
Expresses sophisticated ideas/information/feelings using a sophisticated repertoire of vocabulary
Organises and structures his or her presentation using an effective range of strategies to engage the audience
Achieves the purpose of his or her presentation
Listens to questions/feedback, responds perceptively and, if appropriate, elaborates with further ideas and information

By acknowledging this success criteria in all subjects, we can begin to develop our assessment of effective oracy skills throughout the curriculum. One way this can be adopted is through summative presentations. Tasking students with summarising and presenting the information that they have acquired throughout the topic not only encourages their collaboration skills, but can then be used to support retrieval practice for the remainder of the group, whilst providing a specific formative assessment for those in the group. Whilst these presentations take place, another group could be peer assessing them using the above criteria. Alternatively, this can be done by the class teacher in a more reduced format.

CASE STUDY 4 – ORACY IN THE PRIMARY CURRICULUM

Laura Baxter is an experienced teacher and English specialist at Woodlands Primary School in Birkenhead, where she is a member of the senior leadership team (SLT). With a background in drama and a masters in creative practice, oracy has always been of interest to her.

Having worked as an associate lecturer at Edge Hill University; as a creative facilitator for Creative Partnerships and as a freelance drama advisory teacher (providing bespoke drama projects and CPD across Merseyside), Laura has considerable experience of planning and facilitating learning opportunities.

My school is in a very deprived area and makes more than the average number of referrals to SALT (speech and language therapy). We recognise that good oracy skills are vital and a reliable indicator of success in later life. This solved the first issue of any whole-school project championing change – staff buy in. It was not a hard sell, as staff recognise that many of our children currently have poor oracy skills.

Over the last four to five years, I have been slowly putting things in place:

1. A few years ago, I introduced SLANT to my phase, as a way of helping children develop their listening skills – an important part of oracy.

2. Several years ago, as a school, we adopted the Talk for Writing (T4W) approach, although the oral retelling element is used more regularly in EYFS and KS1 than KS2.

3. More recently, we had also looked at developing Philosophy for Children (P4C) across the school after an excellent trainee teacher had implemented it successfully and led a staff meeting for us.

4. To allow staff to build in opportunities for developing oracy, our foundation curriculum has been reduced (in terms of hours for each subject).

5. Furthermore, after delivering a staff meeting on oracy at a local school, I had set up dates/topics for cross-school debating in KS2, in what we hope will be an annual occurrence.

Significant groundwork laid, and having personally completed training from Voice 21, I led the first of a series of CPD sessions planned on the subject of oracy.

This first session was an introduction – what is oracy?/why should we teach it?/how can we teach it?/a discussion around progression. Within this session, I outlined the two different ways of harnessing oracy in the classroom:

- learning to talk (outcome)
- learning through talk (process).

As teachers, we are very used to enabling children to learn through talk and setting up opportunities to discuss with talk partners and maybe small groups, but when it comes to whole-class 'discussion', we usually revert to hands up and the teacher takes charge.

There are several opportunities and techniques that we can adopt in the primary setting that can be utilised throughout students' academic journey. Opportunities include:

- school council
- acting as guides for visitors and parents
- purposeful debates both in the classroom and through clubs
- No Pens Day
- World Speech Day
- assemblies where students are encouraged to discuss their achievements

Techniques that can be adopted to promote these skills and develop communication include:

Talking tokens

Children are given a number of tokens before the discussion and have to spend them every time they talk. Once they've spent them all, they can't make any more contributions. Quieter members of the class may be encouraged to join in so that they can spend their tokens.

Lego bricks

These can help children to visualise that other people's ideas can be incorporated into their own – they can build on other people's ideas. When a child says something that builds onto the previous point, they can add a brick. A new tower is started when a new line of enquiry begins – providing a visual record of whether children are successfully listening to others and building on their ideas.

Wool/Spider's web

The end of the wool is held by the child who starts the discussion, and they pass the ball on to the next person who contributes. Each time someone new talks, they are passed the wool. Again, this provides a visual record of the discussion – shows how frequently people are contributing.

To summarise: an approach to establishing oracy in primary schools...

Stage 1
Prepare school to embed oracy across the curriculum – deliver CPD introducing some simple strategies, the 4 strands and discuss progression. Consider as a staff what you already do that works and look at areas for development – action plan for the next stage.

Stage 2
A closer look at the 4 strands and introduce assessment structure. Decide as a staff how you will assess – is there mileage in grouping similar children to identify strengths/areas for development (aka APP style) or do you want to complete in-depth assessments for individuals?

Stage 3
Staff begin to plan regular opportunities for developing oracy skills and implement some of the strategies introduced earlier. CPD – planning an oracy-focussed sequence of lessons.

Stage 4
Monitoring/supporting staff with planning and teaching sequences. During learning walks check that sentence structures are displayed in classrooms but more importantly are used by children. Are children listening to others and building on from what they're saying?

Stage 5
Sharing good practice and planning next steps as a school.

Establishing oracy in primary schools

HOW ORACY SKILLS SUPPORT CLASSROOM MANAGEMENT

A wonderful fact to reflect upon, that every human creature is constituted to be that profound secret and mystery to every other.

Charles Dickens, *A Tale of Two Cities*

Introducing oracy skills into the classroom can often be threatened by misconceptions and apprehension surrounding the promotion of peer-to-peer dialogue in the classroom. Maintaining a silent classroom in order to learn and retain knowledge should never be treated as the only possible strategy. If that were truly the case, science practical lessons and physical education would result in bedlam. In 2013, Norwegian May Britt Postholm published a paper that reflected on the research findings of studies into classroom management.

A study carried out by the American researchers Anderman et al. (2011) shows that several factors may impact pupil motivation for schoolwork, and hence their learning. This study comprises teaching and pupil perceptions of the teaching in social studies and natural science. Different subjects have been described as representing different communities with their 'histories, pedagogical traditions and status' (Grossman & Stodolosky, 1994, p. 182), but the researchers in this study state that the conditions and matters that are highlighted may apply across subjects. The pupils perceive teacher support, teacher expectations that they should understand and the social climate in the class as important in their learning process. The teachers who participated in the study demanded understanding through the use of searching questions in dialogues with the pupils, and they supported their pupils by asking open questions. At the start of teaching sessions the teachers presented key concepts and warned pupils about common mistakes. In addition to supporting the pupils in the language process, importance is attached to teachers establishing and maintaining a good relationship [with] the pupils. The pupils are encouraged to ask for help, and the teachers also show that they are enthusiastic about their subject. The teachers display interest in the pupils, an interest that also includes pupil life outside the classroom, and they use humour in their teaching. If the pupils' behaviour needs to be corrected, this is done discreetly so that the flow of the teaching is not disrupted. The study shows the importance of teachers being attentively present in their teaching, and that they are able to quickly understand what is happening, preferably before it happens. The teachers are also active parties in the process when the pupils are working in groups; they remind pupils so they are mindful of the time at their disposal and they support the pupils when they ask for help. In the conclusion of the article, the researchers state that what they have called 'supporting understanding' may promote the pupils' cognitive engagement, establishment and maintenance of good relations which may promote their emotional involvement, and that classroom management may contribute to good behaviour. (Postholm, 2013)

Postholm stresses that 'the use of language in dialogues with other pupils and the teachers is an important tool that creates an interaction between individuals and the environment they live and act in.'

Tips for the classroom

- *The enforcement of expectations is key.* The more that these routines are embedded and reinforced, the more students will begin to intrinsically acknowledge and perform acceptable standards of behaviour.

- *Allow students to take ownership.* In order to gain more of a collective ownership of these expectations, ensure that they are constructed and discussed as a class. Model the requirements for discussions through a facilitated discussion of acceptable and unacceptable behaviour during these tasks. The ability to instil involvement of participants will have more of a positive impact than a dictatorial approach to establishing expectations.

- *Don't avoid the noise.* Embrace the idea that there needs to be noise in your classroom in order to demonstrate effective communication, and be aware that noise levels can easily rise, not because of students deviating from your expectations, but because it naturally happens when people are attempting to create a dialogue in a loud environment.

- *Build up students' skills.* The ability to demonstrate effective oracy skills may need to be scaffolded in some circumstances. By approaching explicit teaching of oracy in a segmented and developing manner, you are building up the confidence and capabilities of your learners.

- *It's ok to start off small.* In the chapter that focusses on monologic and dialogic teaching strategies, it's acknowledged that it is more than acceptable to adopt both approaches and to adapt your approach based on contextualisation.

- *Timing is key.* There are several strategies that practitioners can adopt in order to end the conversations in the classroom. Whether this be vocalising their request, or raising their hand, another common method is the countdown. In any case, the ability to provide students with time to finish off their conversations is integral to ensuring there are no continued discussions. Think about how you feel when someone interrupts your conversation or deflects your focus before you have finished your train of thought. The lack of time to finish off conversations can lead to anger or frustration, which can then act as a catalyst to deviant behaviour.

- *Remain calm and composed.* This behaviour may often lead to a similar or at least simplistic response (which itself could exacerbate the situation, depending on how you react). A sharp and vocalised confrontation will provoke further reaction or cause fear. Fear doesn't breed respect, so this should never be perceived as a positive. There are, however, circumstances where this fear could indicate a fear of failure or disappointment. This is likely to result in a more heightened emotional response.

Incorporating restorative practice

It is worthwhile considering the circumstances where restorative practise can be implemented to address a situation. Engaging students in restorative practice as a preliminary form of disciplinary action can help to resolve infractions, including:

- interpersonal conflict
- verbal or physical conflicts that may have taken place

- property damage (graffiti or deliberate acts of vandalism)
- harassment and cyberbullying
- bullying (physical or verbal)
- theft
- persistent class disruption.

Inclusion of this approach arises from a recognition of the consequences of actions and the understanding that deviant behaviour can often result in harm due to the choices that have been made. This contrasts with punitive justice, which focusses more on the rules that have been broken. The table below attempts to compare the two more intrinsically:

Punitive	Restorative
Deviant behaviour is acknowledged on the breaking of school rules and a defiance of expectations.	The focus is more on the harm that has been done and the recognition that there could be an unconscious contributing factor to the issue.
The approach is specifically focussed on establishing guilt and then attributing a punishment.	There is a necessity to consider the feelings and responsibilities of all impacted individuals and how the situation could be resolved.
The aim is to ensure that the discipline forces the harmful behaviours to cease and that there is an escalation in restrictive and/or exclusionary consequences.	The focus of the intervention goes beyond the event and instead attempts to recognise the root causes of any deviant behaviour. These are then considered and discussed alongside potential positive changes in behaviour.
The interventions that take place are typically decided on by an authority figure with no opportunity to negotiate or consider an alternative.	The emphasis is more on the collaboration and triangulation of those who have been directly impacted by the event in order to consider the needs of all involved.
The concept of accountability is reserved for the receipt of punishment.	Accountability is founded on the ability to take responsibility for choices or actions that have been made.
Imposed punitive consequences can often be perceived as shaming and stigmatising the perpetrator.	Restorative practice considers the ability of the individual to recognise the consequences of their actions and to grow as a result of the experience.

The prospect of introducing restorative practice in a school is often shrouded in misconceptions. Whether looking at it in terms of delivery or intention, it is easy to forget that it can be an effective method for ensuring cohesion between participants. When it comes to behaviour management and supportive strategies, the intention behind restorative practice is to engage with fundamental oracy skills to promote a calm and inclusive setting. Although schools may begin to approach oracy and its implementation with the intention of developing academic potential, the ability to communicate effectively is actually a predominant approach to effective behaviour management. To incorporate restorative practice into your setting, two key skills are needed:

Oracy

To address the problems that have occurred, the recipient needs to demonstrate a cognitive ability in order to articulate the problems.

Social and Emotional

Whether this is the ability to understand the issue and process an emotional response to the event, or even the ability to handle being in close proximity to an individual in a purposeful dialogue, it is important to consider all of the factors that could consequently affect the outcome of the discussion.

There are certain open-ended questions/statements that can be used to provoke a reflective response in the participant when approaching restorative justice. These include:

- Can you tell me what happened?
- Explain to me how it happened.
- What role did you play in the events?
- Was anyone else affected by what you chose to do?
- How did this affect them?
- What could you do to make things better?

If we consider historical interpretations of behaviour management in the classroom, we can't help but be presented with the image of the stern headmaster and the intimidating school mistress. In a profession plagued by its past, the use of corporal punishment in teaching may be a distant memory, but it is still a stigma that brings with it a particular perception of how a teacher is expected to present themselves.

The idea is often promoted that all teachers need to be authoritarian to maintain control of the classroom, with statements such as 'don't smile until Christmas' being embedded into contemporary interpretation of effective behaviour management. Fortunately, through professional development, a plethora of research and the incorporation of realistic expectations of students and staff, there is now more of a distinction between fear and respect.

Fear and respect are two completely different entities. With respect, an individual is driven by self-belief and a desire to succeed. With fear, the individual is driven by force and is typically reluctant. There are several contributing factors in the distinction between the two, including:

- response to negative communication
- a person's interpretation of the volume and tone of voice
- a person's emotional response to the dialogue
- a person's self-drive and next actions as a result of the communication.

This is similar to the reasoning behind the use of titles and surnames in schools. Students are often hesitant about the use of first names in the classroom because it might indicate a lack of respect, and teachers are often reluctant because of the sense of overfamiliarity first names can create. Avoiding first names does not mean that we are attempting to create generic automatons, but arises more from our need to embed simple strategies for respectful communication as early as possible.

Communicating with other stakeholders

It's not just our ability to interact with colleagues and students that forms the foundations of our ability to encourage the learning of our students. For successful development, stakeholders need to be involved in the dialogue, promoting open channels of communication for all parties. Depending on the circumstances of the student, there could be a number of agencies or stakeholders that need to be kept in an open channel of communication regarding care and intervention for the individual.

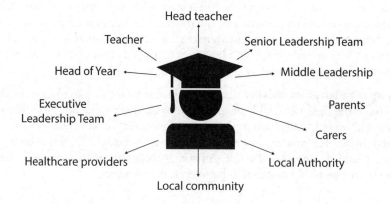

Most of the stakeholders mentioned above (and many more also) are involved in a professional capacity. This means that communication and dialogue with these agencies is often fact-based and rationalised.

Emotional responses that are commonly attributed to parents or carers need particular consideration to ensure that strong parental involvement is maintained, thereby providing open channels of communication that work in the best interest of the individual. The most effective way to support a student, particularly one who may be exhibiting more deviant behaviour, is to ensure that contact is made with the parent or carer.

Trust and rapport are built on transparency.

Even if the concern is not reciprocated, the very recognition of our concern or attempt to rectify a situation could play a substantial role in the student's perception of our capacity to care. Phone calls can often be difficult, particularly if the message is a negative one, and it is important to recognise specific techniques and tips that could prevent a breakdown in communication from occurring.

Top tips for communicating with parents and carers

- When making contact with parents, check that you do so at a suitable time. If you cannot, arrange depending on the purpose of the call.

- Ensure that parents will be able to understand the conversation without your being perceived as patronising. You may require a translator, or alternatively you may need to ensure that you check for comprehension. This information can often be gathered via the initial student application.

- Keep calm and prepare in advance. If the conversation is negative, it is the facts that should take precedence. Avoid exaggeration or hyperbole.

- Consider your own frame of mind. If you are emotionally involved, you may need to take some time prior to the phone call so that you can remain factual and professional. We are all human, so it is important that we stick to the main objective of the conversation.

- Consider the purpose of the conversation and whether a face-to-face meeting would be more beneficial than a phone call.

- If you are meeting a parent, ensure that you prepare for the meeting and arrange a meeting room to ensure that you won't be disturbed. You should also consider whether it would be beneficial to include a colleague in the meeting.

- Ensure that you are demonstrating effective listening in the dialogue and that you are considering your responses carefully.

- A positive rapport is key. Building a relationship with stakeholders in a student's education ensures that a positive atmosphere is built through open channels of communication.

- Don't become lost in the negative. The most rewarding conversations for a parent or carer are those that highlight the positive choices their child has made. As practitioners, we can often be consumed by the necessity to conduct the negative phone calls. Ensuring that we maintain positive communication will have a positive effect on our own professional wellbeing.

Sometimes, channels of communication can break down or not come to fruition. Acknowledging and preparing for these circumstances can help in the establishment or development of dialogue to support the learner.

Language barriers

With the percentage of EAL students in certain demographics increasing, issues regarding the ability to communicate with family members can arise. Often, the student can exhibit more capabilities in English than their relatives because of the student's integration in English-based educational settings. With language comprehension providing the foundations of communication, this can lead to a substantial issue. Strategies to consider would include:

- liaising with the local authority to establish a possible translation service

- establishing an understanding of languages spoken by staff members on site – this can help when dealing with emergency situations and those that require urgent attention.

- offering evening classes to parents in foundational spoken language skills in order to not only develop their own abilities, but also to establish a relationship.

Lack of understanding

It can sometimes be intimidating for parents who may have been less academically able to approach certain topics or communication with schools. Often a lack of understanding can result in a lack of confidence in being able to engage in a dialogue without fear of reprisal or prejudice. Recognition of this factor is thus completely dependent on the topic of conversation and the objective. To provide support in this situation, it is advisable to:

- Keep in constant communication with all stakeholders in a variety of forms. Ensuring channels are used on a frequent basis will provide less of an anomaly if you wish to engage with them.

- Ensure clarity, but in a way that avoids a condescending manner. It would be helpful in certain circumstances, like parents' evening, to provide supporting documents that can be referred to later.

- Summarise the topic of conversation to ensure that all parties are fully aware of what was discussed and what the next steps are.

Lack of motivation/Inconvenience

Although there are unfortunately scenarios where you may have to deal with disengaged stakeholders, this shouldn't necessarily be interpreted as a lack of motivation concerning the learner's education. Sometimes a lack of motivation can imply that it is less likely that plans will be altered or patterns changed to suit any requirements or requests from the academic setting. This can arise with parents or carers who do not attend parents' evening, as well as with those for whom contact may be difficult because of work commitments. These circumstances do not necessarily imply neglect and should never be automatically assumed to be such, but there are strategies that can be incorporated into common practice that will encourage communication:

- Parents' evening should not be the only form of communication that some parents have with class teachers. If a student is not exceptional or in need of behavioural intervention, it is easy for those 'invisible students' to also have 'invisible parents'. Incorporating other forms of communication such as newsletters and emails will ensure that parents or carers remain in the loop and are aware of all meetings well in advance.

- Preparation is key, and notification should be provided for meetings or events well in advance. If these times or dates are not accessible, a phone call, video call or face-to-face meeting should be offered as an alternative.

CASE STUDY 5 – A SENIOR LEADER'S PERSPECTIVE

Sam Strickland is the principal of a large all-through school and has helped to guide its GCSE results from the bottom 20% nationally to the top 20%, and A level outcomes to the top 5% nationally. Sam began his teaching career as a history teacher in Bedfordshire, having completed his postgraduate certificate in education (PGCE) in secondary history at the University of Cambridge under Christine Counsell. His career quickly accelerated and he became head of history and classics. He then moved on to become a lead professional and worked for a SCITT (School Centred Initial Teacher Training) consortium. In 2015 Sam served as an associate principal, with GCSE and A level results under his tenure receiving commendation from the Department for Education (DfE), Nick Gibb and the SSAT (the Schools, Students and Teachers Network). Sam then served as a vice principal, where he directly oversaw student care, the sixth form and the curriculum, and served as the safeguarding lead for an entire trust. The organiser of ResearchED Northampton, he is a leading voice in the current conversation in education. He has had educational resources and research published and has delivered courses nationally.

To speak or not to speak, that is the question.

The role and purpose of oracy has been an area of educational practice that has been hotly contested and debated over the years, with much written on the efficacy of pupil verbal engagement in lessons. The range of debate and approaches has moved from 'do not let pupils speak' at its most controlling to limiting teacher voice so pupils direct the learning themselves at the more liberal end of the spectrum. A challenge for any school and any teacher is finding the right balance and interplay, so that pupils speak at the right moments and about the right things.

When we consider how education has shifted more recently, the new in-vogue approach has seen a regurgitation of more traditional teaching methods and an acknowledgement again that teacher voice is important.

There is also a rejuvenated recognition that pupils need to remember information, under the banner of 'knowledge begets knowledge' (E.D. Hirsch), and store this in their long-term schema. Schools like School 21 have been heralded for their approach to oracy, which has seen their results flourish.

At the core of the matter we need to ask the key question, as we always do for any approach, why? Why do we want our teachers to engage their pupils in oracy orientated approaches to their learning? What benefit does this serve? How does this help learning? If we are truly committed to a knowledge-rich approach, then research would show that oracy plays a huge role in building a pupils' long-term schema. Pupils, if they repeat and cite the same piece of information anywhere between six to ten times out loud, are more likely to remember information long term.

So, what can be done to support the teaching of oracy? There are a number of key approaches that can make a huge difference to lesson delivery, pupil knowledge retention and the overall ability of our pupils to speak. I would like to share a few strategies that I feel do make a difference, as follows:

Choral Chanting

For any given lesson, the teacher really should know precisely what powerful knowledge they want their class to know and why. Going into a lesson, a teacher should have identified three to five key pieces of knowledge; this may well come under the guise of Tier 2/3 vocabulary words. If our pupils are to truly remember these words, then they should say them out loud, coupled with their definition/meaning. The more they say these words, using choral chanting as an approach (i.e. the teacher says then the pupils repeat), then the greater the chances are that the pupils will transfer this knowledge from their working memory to their long-term schema.

Full Sentences

Doug Lemov calls this SHAPE. Whatever way you want to refer to this, however, the key is that pupils respond to a question with a full answer. All too often, if we ask pupils a question we receive at best a short or one-word answer and at the worst a grunt, a mumble or the endless use of 'like' and 'init'. We should not accept or allow this. If we hold high expectations, then we should insist on a full, comprehensive answer. So, for example, if we were to ask our class what is 12 × 12, we should not accept 144 as the answer. Whilst the answer itself is correct, the response is lazy. We should instil in our pupils that we want them to say '12 × 12 equals 144'. Ideally, the pupil should add 'sir' or 'miss' onto the end of their answer. You can then engage the class in chorally chanting this response so the whole class is engaged. Why would we do this? Ultimately, we are trying to teach our pupils to fully articulate their answers. In doing so, they are more likely to remember the information/knowledge. It also comes across that the pupil is in command of the knowledge. A positive by-product of this approach is that pupils will learn to articulate and enunciate their words and sentences, which is key to their future lives.

Retrieval Approaches

The efficacy of retrieval practice has been debated by many educationalists. However, retrieval practice does allow pupils to engage in oracy. For example, you may want your class to verbally tell you all they know about a topic, event, formula, etc. You could ask your class to close their books, think about the characterisation of Mr Birling from *An Inspector Calls*, as an example, and then the pupils have to tell the class all that they know about this character in 30 seconds. There are many recall games you can play which employ the use of oracy.

The beauty of approaches like the ones I have shared with you is that they are directed by the teacher, who remains the expert in the room. A clear use of questioning, timings and well-defined parameters for the pupils will allow them to engage in oracy whilst also allowing the teacher to expertly manage the classroom.

CHANGING THE DIALOGUE

One of the key reasons why oracy must play a fundamental role in the education and development of young people is the necessity to relate this skill to everyday life.

Remember those conversations that most practitioners dread?

The interrogative statement goes along the lines of: 'What are we studying this for?' As a practitioner, you long (and quietly deserve) to reference integral moments where the knowledge students have acquired can reflect everyday situations. Unfortunately, for some students exposure to these concepts has been somewhat limited to specific questions that were laid out by an exam board. These students weren't able to formulate an understanding through logic and hypothetical reasoning; nor were they able to acquire knowledge from appreciation and intrigue. Instead, their responses were more formulaic and stagnant. The concept of critical thinking was reserved for those classed as 'higher ability', and the term 'scaffolding' meant a prescriptive sentence with 'insert word here' that they were expected to recite.

Whether these were the few or the sum, we owe it to all to reflect on this statement and ensure that such situations don't occur in the future.

Don't be afraid to start off small.

Focus on developing aspirational learners

Every art and every inquiry, and similarly every action and choice, is thought to aim at some good; and for this reason the good has rightly been declared to be that at which all things aim.

Aristotle

In 1999, Moon's 'Map of Learning' illustrated a clear identification of the steps required for students to develop reflective techniques to support transformational learning. In Moon's theory, one of the strongest reflection points that anyone can achieve is succinctly linked to their aspirational goals. The principle behind the theory focusses on the interpretation of varying levels of reflection and how this can affect cognitive development. Moon believed that students experienced the following five stages:

- noticing
- making sense
- making meaning
- working with meaning
- transformative learning.

The fundamental principles of the approach focus on the idea that as soon as learners begin to develop meaning and concentrate on inference and interpretation, there is a distinct shift from surface learning to a deeper learning. This then allows a shift from memorisation to retention to occur.

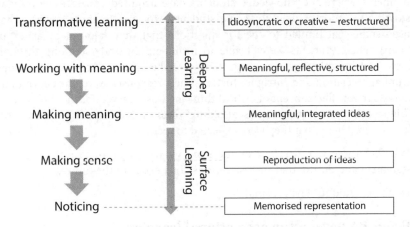

Thus, when we encourage students through aspirational goals, we are supporting them in their reflection on their goals and outcomes, shifting their perspectives from short-term 'wins' to considering a bigger picture.

We as practitioners are not always able to control the experiences and interactions that take place outside of the classroom. Each individual student needs to be recognised as an individual with their own drive, their own ambition and their own attitudes to academia. If we consider what effect it would have on students if they were able to communicate their aspirations with confidence, it is clear that there would be a development of general self-esteem, self-efficacy and independent motivation.

According to the EEF, the principle behind aspiration interventions and research around them came about as a result of the belief that the raising of aspirations is 'often believed to incentivise and improve attainment'. However, the concept of developing aspirations in students is often misjudged and misinterpreted. As most students already possess high aspirations (to some degree), whether this is embraced or veiled, the concept of what that individual wants to do as a career is often already bubbling beneath the surface. The EEF points out that 'much underachievement results not from low aspiration but from a gap between aspirations and the knowledge, skills and characteristics required to achieve them' (Education Endowment Foundation, 2018).

Although there is a lack of compelling evidence to link the development of aspirations to knowledge and learning, one thing that the consideration of aspirations does allow is the ability to provide an alternative perspective – to encourage students to engage in a long-term goal that is achievable, with high hopes and realistic expectations.

It is clear that the ability to mould our language to illustrate life post-academia is imperative when we consider how to re-engage the disengaged. Students need to be exposed to the potential opportunities and situations that exist outside of the classroom, so that we are facilitating the acquisition of valuable life-long skills.

Incorporating aspiration into your lessons

- When introducing a new topic, contextualise the learning. Allow students to see:
  - Why this topic is so significant
  - How the skills can be utilised in day-to-day life
  - Any wider reading that can be done to promote curiosity and further investigation
- Encourage summative dialogue at the end of each unit to cement the key information that will need to be retained. Allow students to consider this in both long-term and short-term planning and summary.
- There are some schools in the UK who have really embraced the concept of developing aspirations to improve student work ethos. In these schools, the concept of developing long-term goals is one that is instilled in students from their arrival into the establishment. They are encouraged to aim high and focus on the bigger picture as opposed to the academic outcomes.

A lot of time and effort is used by schools to demonstrate how they are integrating career opportunities and post-academic options into their curriculum. A useful strategy is to <u>lead with</u> this concept, instead of the inclusion being perceived as an 'add on'. Post-academic opportunities should be addressed and referenced at the start so that students can relate their internal learning to external relevance.

By changing 'preparing for your exams' to 'preparing for your job application', or by explaining the required oracy skills for a task by comparing it to their college interview, students will be able to think past their exams and their academic cocoon. More often than not, this could easily become intertwined with the approach of changing the mindset of the students. However, it's much more straightforward than the idea of allowing students to look further into the future.

Whereas Dweck's (2016) concepts of mindset appear to focus more on the power of suggestion and the ability to adopt a more positive approach alongside the consequences of such, this dialogue focusses on a realistic picture of the definitive as opposed to the possibility. This reasoning does not depend on the idea of changing a culture or appealing to self-confidence, but more on the acknowledgement of future moments and the recognition of the consequences of being underprepared for the life experiences one might experience next.

In order to develop a more aspirational approach, and ensure that students are prepared, a substantial amount of time and energy within their time in school needs to be dedicated to developing aspirational goals and the ability to articulate post-academia aims. This can be done during lessons that focus specifically on personal, social and health education, or even in a subject-specific lesson if you would like to encourage a dialogue that is based around engagement with your particular subject. On a more personal reflection level, the questions would include a chronological progression of key life events:

- What do you want to do at college?
- What part-time job would you be interested in doing whilst you studied?
- What would you like to do after college?
- Is there a particular job that you would be interested in?
- Where do you see yourself in five to ten years' time?

Often the inclusion of these questions can be seen as intimidating and disconcerting; the concept of being asked to write these aspirations down can be portrayed as cementing or contractually agreeing to these statements, which can often lead to 'push-back' or disengagement from students, particularly those who are less fixed in their confidence around next steps. This apprehension cannot be portrayed as a negative, as it needs to be clear that there is no 'right answer' to these questions. By using oracy skills to engage with this topic, you are more likely to encourage more developed responses from students. The knowledge that they can have a discussion regarding their current viewpoint will enable them to build their confidence and their belief that achieving their aspirations is possible. Communicating these ideas is the first step to developing the knowledge that their goals can actually happen without fear of failure or force.

Aim high and don't compromise

Years ago, teacher training providers and practitioners alike had a 'recipe' for the perfect lesson. This lesson was predominantly based on the misconception that engagement led to learning – that learning and knowledge acquisition are by-products of a lesson tailored to the interests of a specific cohort.

Slowly, the profession has begun to acknowledge the idea that tailoring knowledge can actually funnel and have a detrimental impact on achieving full potential. It almost eradicates the opportunity to be exposed to the new and the unknown, instead sheltering students in the common and the familiar. Students need to find topics and concepts difficult. They need to be guided through how to articulate their critical thinking and develop their hypotheses.

CASE STUDY 6 – ORACY IN DIVINITY

Marie Mulcrow has had numerous roles in her twenty years' experience of teaching that include head of year, spiritual leader in sixth form, second in department, progress leader, and head of department. She is currently working at Saint Martin's Catholic Academy.

Our mission at Saint Martin's Catholic Academy is for pupils to learn '[t]he best that has been thought and said' (Mathew Arnold) and to know that they are loved. 'A new commandment I give you: Love one another. As I have loved you, so must you love one another' (John 13:34), combining our mission to educate our children in body, faith and mind.

Divinity is the 'core of the core curriculum' at Saint Martin's (Pope St John Paul II). Placing divinity at the core of the curriculum helps us to fulfil our mission to educate the whole person in discerning the meaning of their existence, since '[d]ivinity is concerned not only with intellectual knowledge but also includes emotional and affective learning. It is in the mystery of the Word made flesh that the mystery of what it is to be human truly becomes clear. Without [d]ivinity, pupils would be deprived of an essential element of their formation and personal development, which helps them attain a vital harmony between faith and culture' (Religious Education Curriculum Directory, p. 4).

Results last year were 87% 9–4 from our students in year 10. How do we do this?

I am lucky that I have inherited a team of experts in direct instruction in divinity. The thought and planning behind the curriculum is crucial in developing AT1 skills of knowledge and understanding, AT2 skills of engagement and response and AT3 skills of analysis and evaluation.

One way in which I do this is through Doug Lemov's 'Call and Response' or, as I call it, 'Choral response'. So what do this mean in practice?

A well-thought-through curriculum model developed by @m_blissett, which chronologically focusses on the start of the world with God's Creation in Genesis and journeys through to the New Testament, enables our students to engage with both scripture and faith, stories and tradition.

Our knowledge booklets are deep and theological and encourage a thirst for more, with students in year 7 raising questions that I had previously taught to year 12 on the existence of God. If God created the world *ex nihilo* (from nothing), who created God? Is it better for humans to have free will or for God to have created us to always do good? I joke with my students that they are really semi necessary beings (God is the Necessary Being), but their knowledge and insight at times cause me to amaze that they are more than just contingent beings.

So for each lesson, students are given key vocabulary to learn in advance. Five words to learn over a week might not initially sound like much, but the impact builds an invisible essay as more words are added each week, as well as passages from scripture. I encourage students to put a timer of fifteen minutes on at home, and they verbally chant each word and the definition for three minutes at a time, moving from the first to the fifth word. After fifteen minutes, they spend five minutes – one minute on each word – recapping, and then write out the definitions of the words to ensure that the recall becomes part of their long-term memory. When they come into class, we warm up for five minutes and then the choral response of each word is said. I survey the room to ensure all are involved and then will randomly ask students through cold calling the definition of a key word. This then becomes powerful knowledge when dealing with big questions such as 'Who is God?' and 'How have things gone wrong for human beings?'

As the lessons build with further learning and retrieval of knowledge, I ask students, with key words on the board, to tell the story so far in five minutes in a written account. This enables me not only to see the impact of retrieval and recall of key vocabulary AT1 skills, but also to use a range of scripture passages.

Using Rosenshine's principles of direct instruction, I ask students to consider the following questions: Who is God?', 'What does God want from us?', 'What did God do to make this possible?', 'How have things gone wrong for human beings?', 'So far in our story, what has God done to repair the damage?'

In this instance, when I fed back to the class for each question, I broke down the percentage between boys and girls to help with research in the classroom. For this class, 17.9 out of 20 was the average mark for boys and 18.6 out of 20 was the average mark for girls. The average mark for the class was 18.25 out of 20, making this a success rate of 91.25% for the class.

This information was then fed back to them alongside our marking crib sheet. On the crib sheet, we focus on the key areas of:

- progress/praise
- missing/incomplete areas
- misconceptions
- SPaG
- presentation
- 'Polaroid moment' – examples of exemplary work in critical thinking.

Such a strong foundation builds pupils' faith, vocabulary and literacy skills in my experience. In December 2019, students were asked: 'What's the difference between religious education at primary school and secondary school?' The response from the students was that more elements of the topic are addressed in a greater depth. Therefore, the amount of content that is provided in secondary schools doesn't necessarily change, but the depth into which these concepts are explored is deeper and more critical.

With the unprecedented COVID-19 situation, how would our strong foundation change? Well, the work we set for our students in lockdown followed the same pattern of 'Do Now', annotating booklets and answering key questions in depth. The prerecording of Microsoft Teams lessons as well as live lessons and online tutorial support enabled retrieval of key vocabulary to be said chorally online.

I asked our students to complete a survey by themselves at home on Microsoft Forms to evaluate their experience of year 7 divinity at Saint Martin's.

The results included:

- 90% of students either agreed or strongly agreed that they made outstanding progress in divinity in comparison to their interpretation of progress in other subjects.

- 78% of students acknowledged that they used the knowledge gained in this subject and were able to transfer this thinking and reference in day-to-day life.

- 87% of students either agreed or strongly agreed with the fact that they have a clear understanding not just of their progress, but also of the next steps in learning that are required for them to improve.

- When asked about their progress scores in comparison to other subjects (to provide me with an area of reflection), 44% of students actually disagreed that their results were best in divinity. To consider this further and in more depth, the next step was to consider which subjects students believed they were performing better in, and what strategies were being incorporated in these circumstances that were the same or different.

- Students found the work challenging (79%), whilst they believed that their work was celebrated through the implementation of positive comments.

One student in my class wrote:

My experience in divinity is great. My teacher is very supportive and we always get positive feedback. We are confident in our Knowledge Organisers, as we do recalling when we say the words and definitions over and over again for a certain amount of time and this really puts it into your head as it is like a song you listen/sing to over and over again and you just can't get it out of your brain.

UNDERSTANDING THE FUNDAMENTAL TEACHING STRATEGIES OF THE CLASSROOM

Every few years there is a mass surge of pedagogical refreshment and reinvention regarding effective teaching and learning strategies. Whether you have attempted the Kagan structures or the acknowledgement of visual, audio and kinaesthetic learning styles, or you've just done something with hats (?!?!), the fact of the matter is that teaching and learning needs to be interpreted to suit what will work best for you as a practitioner and for your cohort of students. The recognition of situational analysis and reflective teaching allows us to consider the strategies that we can use to further expand the learning that is taking place.

Who leads the learning?

The year 2020 appeared to be the year where the proverbial gates of Britain's education strategies were prised open, unleashing a flood of questions and changes that have engulfed all those within the teaching profession. The incorporation of innovative learning strategies alongside the navigation through some of the most surreal uncharted waters that practitioners have ever experienced has definitely rocked the boat of what we could classify as mainstream education strategies.

With the enhanced pressure of target-teaching and the need to ensure that high expectations are consistently met, it is easy to lose sight of the particular needs of our students as we concentrate specifically on the generalised specifications of others. A crucial element to learning for this next generation will be their independent skills and resilience. Although these traits are integral to effective knowledge acquisition, we also need to consider how we can utilise the classroom environment to develop the oracy skills of individual learners.

When preparing for learning, practitioners must consistently provide lessons which ensure that all students make progress and that they are all able to embed their learning into their memory for retrieval later. To do this, the juxtaposition between teacher-led and student-led strategies is constantly revisited by all those hoping to improve their students' progress. With these two approaches appearing to have been locked in a continuous battle for priority during the past decade, it is easy to suggest that the pendulum of expectations swings sporadically between the two on (what feels like) a daily basis.

When we consider all of the scientific research and pedagogical suggestions that have been introduced to develop mastery and automaticity in knowledge acquisition, it is clear that one must be continuously flexible in order to manipulate an arsenal of teaching strategies that cater towards the needs and expectations of the spectators as opposed to those of the student participants.

As a result, the list of aspects to take into consideration prior to even approaching one's planning has become considerably longer. At the same time, most schools across the country have become engulfed in a wave of new and innovative assessment strategies that could potentially act as the 'Cinderella slipper' that we have all been waiting for.

It is easy to begin to opt out of more student-led activities for fear of students not fully understanding or comprehending the learning objectives. The biggest question to answer is this: Are you willing to move from being a practitioner to a facilitator, putting more emphasis on student-led teaching as opposed to teacher-led strategies that may have been previously deemed the 'safe bet'?

Practitioner, facilitator or both?

There are certain factors to consider when establishing the most efficient approach to supporting learning. One factor is the need to strengthen the relationship between teaching and learning by incorporating collaborative opportunities that encourage and enable all pupils to participate. Another focus point is developing pupils' skills of working both independently and in groups depending on the task and expectations; enabling teachers and pupils to move learning forward together through a judicious use of pedagogical strategies.

The primary initiative placed an emphasis on students becoming responsible for their own learning. With some schools and establishments still linking performance management to salary changes, are we ready to place our success into students' hands, though?

These changes have resulted in the need to reinvent the personalised classroom previously outlined by the Department for Education. It specified that the relationship between teaching and learning can be formed through the successful administration of a classroom in which the students have more opportunities to:

> Get involved, be curious, develop interests and call for the help they need. The challenge for pupils is to take responsibility for their own learning; and the challenge for the education system is to engage their instinct to learn.' (DfE, 2014)

In the dawning of the assessment purgatory, where we are caught in fear of misinterpretation or inaccuracy due to a lack of explicit guidance as to a consistent approach, teachers cannot be blamed for beginning to question whether the use of student-led activities would help or in fact hinder the level of progression that appears to be required.

Reasonably, one could argue that by scripting our students and by dictating what can be discovered, we as practitioners are in fact creating a glass ceiling for our students that is preventing them from being confident enough to interpret information in a more unique and evaluative fashion. More and more subjects are increasingly seeing a rise in exam questions which appear to relish the opportunity provided by independent expression.

What the students think

In a short investigation that involved year 7 to year 11, I asked students to explain what they would identify as a positive and a negative for both student-led and teacher-led learning. The students were then asked to identify which one they preferred, as well as their year group and gender.

The results were surprisingly enlightening when it came to understanding student 'wants' and the different strategies available. Despite the fact that we as practitioners are continuously made aware of the benefits of both teacher-led and student-led learning, it is *how* these strategies are approached and implemented in the most efficient and delicate way that is the most intrinsic element to consider.

On reflection, although recording the collected quantitative data provided me with no actual surprises, the collective research did allow me to rethink the approaches and strategies currently in place for these particular students.

To best understand the information, I shall focus on the responses of years 7, 10 and 11. These covers two key transitional phases and the penultimate year of secondary education.

Year 7

The answers provided by these students demonstrated the most reflection in regard to catering for students' needs as opposed to specific management requirements. Although we advocate and emphasise that most activities in the classroom should be student led in order to promote engagement and learning, 72% of this class opted for a teacher-led approach as their specified choice, with 38% of the class specifying that a positive aspect of this approach is that you learn more.

A staggering 74% of students in the classroom listed the social pressures that are placed on the students as the negative for group work.

This, for me, has resulted in a reassessment in how to approach group work in a year 7 classroom. It is understandable that, as a result of going through a significant transitional period, students are apprehensive in regard to collaborative learning strategies because of a lack of social confidence. Therefore, this confidence needs to be built on through the use of strategies such as philosophy circles – an approach that considers development through group discussions and deeper thinking methodologies.

Providing these students with situations that start off as teacher led but gradually offer them more ownership helps them to become more cooperative and confident in their own abilities.

Years 10 and 11

These are the year groups where cumulative planning time is typically considerably longer. All focal points and assessment strategies revolve around the students' impending GCSEs and thus reaching their specified target.

The results between the two year groups were similar to those which emerged from the year 7 class. Despite the fact that the year 10 group has matured somewhat and become more socially confident, their negative perception of the student-led approach appeared to mirror that of the year 7s.

With their entry into the KS4 curriculum, these students have lost a considerable amount of confidence in their own abilities. Despite this, there was a 50% split between the two approaches. The findings were also split in relation to gender. Whereas those who identified as male unanimously expressed a preference towards group work and the student-led approach, 81% of those identifying as girls chose the teacher-led approach, citing their reasons as 'You learn more' (45%), 'You get a better understanding', and 'You get more work done during the lesson'.

These interpretations changed drastically in year 11, when the emphasis is securely placed on students' responsibility for their own learning. As a result, 77% expressed a preference for the student-led approaches that could be made available to them, with the emphasis being placed on the fact that, as a result, they are provided with 'more independence' and allowed to be 'more creative with their thoughts and ideas'.

Overall, the results suggested that despite more students choosing a preference for a student-led approach over classroom learning, 34% of this specific cohort who identified as female specified a preference for the teacher-led approach.

Practical ideas and guidance

When considering how to group your students, preparation is key. The current OFSTED (2019) and Local Education Authority guidelines specifically outline the need to take the following classifications of students into consideration during each stage of the preparation process:

- students classed as pupil premium
- students with special educational needs
- students who are classed as having English as an additional language.

In addition to this, it is likely that your school has also identified further areas of specific focus, such as year 11 boys, or all students teetering on the C/D borderline. As a result of this, preparing for group work can often be a challenging and somewhat daunting experience. When setting up for such a task, it is often a good idea to implement what can only be referred to as the classroom chaos theory.

Often, we as practitioners become so consumed with being effective behaviour managers that fears begin to surface whenever the idea of 'turning the classroom upside down' is even mentioned. Creating a productive, self-focussed, student-led learning environment for which one must perform a mid-lesson classroom rearrangement can often appear unrealistic and time consuming; but it needn't be.

Be safe in the knowledge that there will be times (particularly if your classroom layout requires adjusting) that you may find yourself drowning in a sea of hustle and bustle that can only be compared to a busy market square. This chaos, however, will soon subside as a result of careful management and strategically explained instructions.

When implementing this technique with two key stage 3 classes (mixed ability), I chose to evoke the competitive nature which can be found hiding (or on the surface) of every student. Timing the classes and relaying their time to their 'competition' resulted in a dramatic shift in the amount of time spent in the 'danger zone'. By persevering with the strategy, one year 8 class went from two minutes forty-five seconds to fifty-five seconds on their last attempt.

At this point, it must be acknowledged that adopting a competitive approach within the classroom setting can often be detrimental to the learning of students who may not want to participate because of an acceptance that they will not succeed in their attempt. Therefore, although this strategy has been advocated here, this is more to promote a quick and efficient approach to adopting a tidy classroom as opposed to attempting to encourage students to participate in learning.

Another strategy that can support the provisional embedding of oracy in the classroom is the incorporation of a controlled environment in which students can feel comfortable exhibiting their opinion and perhaps even contributing to a discussion. One effective strategy to act as a catalyst to these discussions is the adoption of the ABC approach.

This can be used to start and encourage any in-class discussion. Although this strategy is more teacher led, it is a good starting point on which to build the foundations of effective communication. The ability to control conflict resolution or expand on a point using a different voice allows for the teacher to serve as the conductor of conversation.

Provisionally, students may need a sentence starter and a way of identifying whether they are agreeing, building on or challenging the statement.

Agreeing

- I agree with…because…
- I would argue the same thing because…
- The reason I agree with…is…
- This is an interesting point because…

Building

- I would like to build on…'s point because…
- I agree with…but I'd like to add…
- In addition to…'s point…

- Building on what...said...
- That is a good argument. However, it could be added...

Challenging

- I disagree with...because...
- I don't think...is right because...
- I would like to challenge this because...
- My own view is different because...
- I believe this statement could be incorrect because...
- I'd like to counter this perspective because...

After these skills and expectations are embedded, the reins can slowly be loosened, with the teacher-led aspects of the conversation slowly waning away to be replaced by the role of the facilitator.

CASE STUDY 7 – USING STORYTELLING AND DRAMA IN THE CLASSROOM

Chris Connaughton is a children's author and playwright who tours extensively to primary schools with his storytelling performances and writing workshops. He is the author of The Beltheron series of fantasy thrillers for upper key stage 2 and key stage 3, and has had plays for young audiences commissioned by Theatre Hullabaloo, The Berry Theatre and Cleveland Theatre Company. As a professional actor, he has played many Shakespearean roles, as well as appearing in Byker Grove and on Button Moon! Info on his educational work and school visits can be found at intextperformance.com.

As a writer for children, a storyteller and performer, I often talk about using storytelling and drama as getting learning in 'under the wire', using it to engage the children so completely that they are absorption machines for information, experience and emotion.

I like to create work which is challenging and complex, but to deliver it in a way in which the child feels comfortable and engaged, a way in which they feel empowered and enabled to join in, speaking their minds and offering opinions in language they may not have been able to use before. I usually aim at least a year group higher than my target audience in terms of themes and vocabulary.

In my own versions of classic tales for younger children in foundation stage and KS1, I sometimes use three or more different words for one thing. ('The gigantic tree was huge. It was enormous, so big that you couldn't see the top.' Or: 'Very carefully, quietly and tentatively, Alice reached up for the key.') Context helps, of course. The setting of a play and the presentation of a particular character often means you can use quite advanced language and ideas, using the story or presentation style as a way to develop vocabulary and meaning.

In this way we can introduce new vocabulary – sometimes challenging, advanced vocabulary – in a way that can be understood by the child, without having to actually explain it to them. You get the meaning in 'under the wire'.

This benefits not only oracy and language either; it can help with confidence and enthusiasm too.

I always remember a boy I met during a day-long visit to a Y5 class some time ago. After watching a performance of Robinson Crusoe in the morning, followed by a Q&A with me (the writer and solo performer of the piece), the class went on to produce diary entries of Crusoe's first day on the island, focussing on the five senses. They then wrote an emotional letter home to a loved one, to be sealed in a bottle, and in role as journalists they interviewed Crusoe for a newspaper article. Finally, in groups, they began to create an annotated map of the desert island. One boy was leaning over the table enthusiastically, coloured marker pens gripped firmly in his fingers, scribbling away on the huge sheet of paper, his tongue sticking out of the side of his mouth in concentration.

'I think you've enjoyed today, haven't you?' I asked him.

'Oh, it's been brilliant,' he said.

'What have you enjoyed most?' I asked.

'I love it because we haven't had to do any work.'

Not only that, but his teacher told me afterwards that he had shown more confidence in speaking up than at any other time that term.

On another occasion, I delivered a day of activities based around a (much shortened) version of *Hamlet*. I was in a school in Redcar. (This is a region of the north-east of England which has suffered hugely both economically and socially in recent years; the catchment area of this particular school was no exception.) At the end of the day a young girl stood up in front of the year group to sing a song she had written that afternoon. It was based on Ophelia's reaction to Hamlet's betrayal. Her voice, frail and piping, hardly reached halfway across the hall, but we all heard every single word, because we were all – children and adults – captivated by the emotion she conveyed in her own words, in her own voice. Halfway through I glanced across at her class teacher to see tears streaming from her eyes. That girl's 'Song for

Ophelia' remains one of the highlights of my 25 years of working in schools.

Of course, this doesn't happen all the time. However, I find that responses like this are not uncommon. I often hear teachers say thing like, 'That is the first time that Jack has put his hand up with an idea all term' or 'Jill never joins in with group discussions, but today we couldn't shut her up!' The teachers are often surprised at this reaction, but we, the practitioners (the actors, writers, storytellers), are not. We recognise the power that performance (and the arts in general) can have on releasing not only ideas, but the ability to speak and communicate those ideas in a safe environment. In real life a performer is often shy or nervous about speaking their mind. Freed from that by playing a role, or having the words of a script to fall back on, they can find a way of expressing an emotion which otherwise might lie unnoticed or misunderstood.

Responses like the ones mentioned above happen regularly enough for me to realise that there is a genuine cause and effect going on here for many children. I believe it is partly the safe space of being able to play a role, to voice an idea or opinion you might ordinarily be too embarrassed or insecure to speak of, and also the fact that context and character allow us to aim high with our ideas and vocabulary so that we are giving our young people access to a rich and varied world of language.

So, don't be scared of your own voice! Tell a story. Act it out. Use it as an excuse to revel in beautiful words and phrases, in a context where the meaning will be understood 'under the wire'. You might find that your children begin to use that language for themselves.

MONOLOGIC OR DIALOGIC APPROACHES TO LEARNING

I never teach my pupils, I only attempt to provide the conditions in which they can learn.

Albert Einstein

In 2015, Ali Jamali Nesari carried out an investigation that considered the distinction between monologic and dialogic teaching strategies. The study concluded that dialogism and its components are 'undoubtably the most appropriate method of teaching in the modern world'. It also concluded that:

> The modern day student is presented with a lot of information and communication tools which can be used for learning any and all material. Hence, regarding the benefits of dialogic concepts for learning and teaching environments it can be said that the learning process cannot simply go on using traditional methods since these bore the students rapidly and decrease the efficiency of the teaching process. (Nesari, 2015, p. 647)

Although Nesari completely disregards monologic teaching methods as a viable option in the twenty-first century, it is important to recognise the reasoning behind this investigation in the first place: it is about the acquisition of skills that students can take with them into the workplace and beyond.

Monologic teaching can be compared to attending a university lecture. The lack of interaction and the unidirectional approach is one that students will be exposed to whether or not they choose to go on to further education and/or work in a professional capacity that provides additional training or large-cohort meetings. Students need to develop the ability to consume the information being distributed whilst using their own metacognition to reflect on and apply reasoning and relativity to the information they are being exposed to.

When we contrast the monologic approach with dialogic teaching, we can identify the advantages and disadvantages of each style and carefully consider how to utilise them effectively in our own environment.

Monologic teaching

The task of the modern educator is not to cut down jungles, but to irrigate deserts.

C.S. Lewis

Amid the fanfare of innovative teaching and learning strategies and their range of techniques that could resemble a technicoloured dream coat, it is easy to become overwhelmed by the breadth and depth of strategies available.

We, as practitioners, are often quick to judge the idea of 'teaching' as opposed to 'engaging' students. One crucial point to remember when considering which styles or approaches will work well in our classroom is to err on the side of caution whenever we hear the word 'engagement'. Often, this can be like a poison in the context of learning and can lead to students having their development hindered. Teachers can sometimes choose to avoid exposing their students to concepts that have been deemed 'less exciting', 'too challenging' or 'not of any personal interest' given the students' age, gender or social/cultural demographic.

Although we may deem a solely monologic approach to be dry, crass and a one-person show, it is an approach that has proved to work. In 2006, Kirschner, Sweller and Clark conducted an investigation into the difference between approaching knowledge acquisition through guided learning (where the teacher uses direct instruction) and learning that is more inquisitive (based on constructionist, experiential and problem-based approaches). They concluded that, despite the preference of the learner for the more problem-based approaches, it was actually the direct instruction method that produced the best knowledge acquisition.

Although this authoritarian approach comes under frequent scrutiny for its lack of 'thinking skill development' (Edwards, 1981), the use of direct instruction can still provide all subjects with the opportunity to lay the foundations on which other methodologies (if desired) can be constructed to enhance and develop the learning acquisition of our students.

The intricacies of direct instruction and monologic teaching styles can bring with them a plethora of useful techniques that can allow students to really engage with their own learning:

- The ability to provide students with small chunks of new information quickly and efficiently in order to develop their knowledge of a particular subject.

- The use of scaffolding that can be provided so that (if used correctly) students are encouraged to expand their responses through support and guidance as opposed to simply 'filling in the blanks'.

- Monologic teaching and direct instruction clearly model the required oracy skills of our learners. When they are done correctly, students are exposed to an appropriate pace, tone and vocalisation of an idea that is shared with a large audience. The opportunity for students to also see someone deal confidently and without remorse with mistakes will allow them to develop confidence in their own communication.

- This methodology can also be used to provide systematic feedback 'en masse'. Engagement with a large group of individuals can be used to support 'whole-cohort feedback' that enables teachers to deal with the most common misconceptions or areas of concern that have arisen in an assessment, for example.

A prime example of this is the delivery of a session on examination feedback and results in lecture format to a whole cohort. It is crucial for a faculty leader to ensure that an entire cohort receives the same message, delivered in the same way, and with emphasis on the same areas of concern or development when considering collective progress. Although all students will need to advance their own development through individual reflection, it could easily be argued that the incorporation of one core platform and delivery will ultimately save time and resources, and will help avoid misconceptions in the long term.

As Matt Bromley pointed out in a SecEd article (2017), there are several supportive techniques that need to be considered to allow monologic teaching strategies to flourish and support development:

1. The contextualisation of **metaphors and analogies** to ensure comprehension through the application of logic and the association to real-life scenarios.

2. The incorporation of **dual coding** to provide additional support to students in the form of images that can be used to guide and support their knowledge retention.

3. The recognition of accurate **pitching** and accessibility to successfully deliver the same key information whilst ensuring that accurate support structures are embedded to encourage the support and guidance required by some.

4. The acknowledgement and incorporation of **reciprocity** in order to further develop learner retention. Although most of the dialogue is likely to come from the teacher, it is still vital to give the students time to relay this information either directly to a teacher or to a peer.

5. The use of effective **models** to demonstrate expectations and requirements. Examples and guidance are key. The opportunity for students to be exposed to cognitive process and the intricacy of formulating a response is crucial in allowing them to develop confidence and articulation of their own.

Monologic teaching summarised

- Information is delivered in more of a lecture-style approach in which key information is distributed by one individual.

- This approach is particularly useful when there is 'missing information' or there are gaps in learning that need to be shared with a large cohort.

- Often, the most effective strategy with this approach is to incorporate time after the session to provide a seminar-style reflection. This additional session can be facilitated by a teacher and can be used to answer any questions or to consider any misconceptions that may have arisen from students not being able to 'talk out their ideas'.

- Instead of questions being delivered to deepen knowledge, the questions are used more to gauge generic and whole-cohort comprehension.

- All conversations are led by the teacher, and students are required to take turns speaking directly to the teacher (typically through questioning) when requested to do so.

  ✓ Suitable for providing subject-specific requirements that are more beneficial for assessments.

  ✓ Can provide supportive 'catch-up' information or the same generic information to an entire cohort.

✗ The information is rarely embedded into substantive knowledge that can be processed in the long-term memory prior to any additional support or approaches.

✗ The concept of mass comprehension is rarely accurate, with no definitive proof that all students have understood the subject matter to the same degree. Some may need to revisit certain areas because of confusion or misinterpretation.

Dialogic teaching

A leader is best when people barely know he exists, when his work is done, his aim fulfilled, they will say: we did it ourselves.

Lao Tzu

To reference Robin Alexander from the Bradford Teachers Project (2019), there are some fundamental goals that demonstrate the effective implementation of dialogic teaching:

1. There is a **collective** approach to addressing tasks where the result isn't necessarily driven by the teacher. By focussing on a group dynamic, there is a higher potential for students to develop their own critical thinking and justification.

2. Evidence of a **reciprocal** dialogue encourages the concepts of challenge and justification by all. By acknowledging a variety of voices, the ability of less confident speakers to share their interpretation becomes more likely as a result of their acknowledgement of a more dynamic interaction.

3. The creation of a **supportive** environment promotes confidence in students to articulate their viewpoints. Although this is typically associated with positive praise by the facilitator, this isn't necessarily the true extent of a supporting environment. Support is a collective concept that is shared by all participants. The ability of students to vocalise their interpretation or reflection without fear of repercussions or negative responses from anyone in the group is crucial for success.

4. Responses are approached in a **cumulative** manner that shows a cohesion between teacher approach and student perception. Despite the fact that the dialogue is one that must be ventured by the students, it is still crucial that the overall objective is navigated by the teacher.

5. Conversation is **purposeful** and drives towards a specific goal. The opportunity for conversations to go on tangents, and for the purpose of the session to be lost in a maze of conversations and deviating exchanges, are plentiful. In a metaphorical sense, the teacher must captain the ship to reach the destination, but the students are the ones providing the power.

As the students begin their adventure in the classroom, it is important that we are utilising these strategies in order to develop their aspirations and to challenge any negative self-perceptions. This is vital when supporting students to re-establish themselves as learners as opposed to spectators.

Dialogic teaching summarised

- The learning is in more of a conversational approach as opposed to a teacher-led discussion. The opportunity for the students to encounter uncertainty allows them to engage in more critical thinking through the formulation of opinions and speculative rationalisation.

- These conversations take place as exploratory talk that encourages students to work through their thought process. In these situations, students are encouraged to make mistakes or to question their own interpretations in order to provide a more collaborative approach to the thought process.

- In these situations, the students are responsible for leading the conversations and for developing their own interpretations. To avoid any misconceptions, the teacher is there to facilitate these conversations by fulfilling an encouraging role. This can be done by agreeing with and continuing to question ideas, or alternatively it can be developed by either providing an alternative consideration or challenging the conversation to deepen the justification and/or the counterarguments.

- Dialogic teaching strategies are instrumental in supporting students to recognise the importance of conversations in a variety of contexts with a variety of audiences.

> ✓ They allow students to develop a deeper understanding of a concept, whilst providing them with the opportunity to vocalise their own interpretations.
>
> ✓ They provide the opportunity for the teacher to facilitate discussion whilst considering individual comprehension.
>
> ✗ In order to work effectively, routines and expectations need to be established straight away. These routines then require embedding to have a substantial effect on the learning ethos of the students.
>
> ✗ It is worth mentioning here that the key stage 2 research that was conducted by the EEF found that one of the biggest criticisms of the incorporation of dialogic teaching strategies in the classroom was that teachers recognised the need for a longer period of time to see true progress (the trial was conducted over the course of a term).

Although we need to recognise the need for and the common use of monologic teaching in the classroom (teacher-led lessons being generally favoured for initial knowledge acquisition), we also need to encourage and not shy away from the prospect of active conversations in the classroom.

CASE STUDY 8 – RAISING THE PROFILE OF ORACY

Lucy Bellingham is a drama teacher, examiner and education consultant who has worked with schools, colleges and theatre companies in London and the midlands for the last 20 years. She is the founder of the company Teaching Drama (www.teachingdrama.org), which provides training and resources for secondary drama teachers.

Several years ago, I worked in an 'Outstanding' academy in East London, as head of performing arts. As a middle manager, I started to do learning walks and lesson observations and noticed that there was hardly any talk in lessons throughout the school. Students were sitting and studying, writing or listening, but there was little debate, discussion or verbal questioning. In performing arts and PE there was more, by nature of the subjects, but throughout the school it was quite different.

I started by doing learning walks around the school, with a specific focus on oracy, and informed staff beforehand. I had a checklist, focussing on opportunities for discussion, questioning, reading aloud, presentations and group work. This was in the form of tick lists to obtain some data. I also spoke to heads of faculties about oracy within their departments. Many of them said that they were reluctant to encourage the development of oracy, as they felt this would lead to a loss of order or control, thus leading to a decline in behaviour. Some also said that they did not know *how* to facilitate debate and discussion confidently. There was definitely resistance from some staff, but SLT still supported the development of oracy, so we went ahead with implementing an oracy strategy over one year.

Our broad aims were:

- to raise the profile of oracy throughout the school (dispel the myth that it is only important in drama!)
- to make oracy more 'visible' in the daily life of the school

- to improve the responses of students when answering questions in lessons (full sentence answers as opposed to one word).

We devised a plan of activities for the year, culminating in our 'Summer of Learning' festival, which ran for three weeks, and made oracy a focus of all the scheduled activities. We implemented the following:

- A drama scheme of work for every year 7 student called 'All About Me'. Every student in year 7 delivered a solo presentation in their drama lesson. Students were fully supported in lessons when planning and rehearsing these. A presentation was modelled at the start of the scheme and students were given detailed feedback throughout. The key aspect of the assessment was speaking without notes, even if it was short. The best presentations were shown informally to parents at the end of the school day, in the drama studio. They were shared at morning staff briefings, when we also talked about how we set up the project. These became regular oracy CPD sessions in staff briefings, lasting five to ten minutes. We also came up with a guide for teachers facilitating presentations in their lessons.

- Debates started happening once a week in the 'atrium' (shared space in the school), at break and at lunchtime. We invited an organisation in to set these up and train key staff to run a debating society. English integrated this into schemes of work at all levels.

- Students from English and drama prepared speeches and monologues which were performed during staff briefings, break and lunchtime. There were mini 'stages' set up around the atrium.

- The year 6 transition day consisted of Shakespeare Day – this was delivered with around 20 Teach First English teachers about to embark on their training year. Small group sessions were delivered to the year 6 students transitioning to year 7. These sessions very much focussed on oracy and were used to develop students' understanding of a Shakespeare play. The day culminated in a performance of the annual Shakespeare production.

- The GCSE drama students did a radio play project with a local theatre company, writing their own plays and performing them live, which were also recorded.

- Student leadership (two students from each class) took part in presentation skills training with members of staff, enabling them to present more confidently in assemblies.

- We ran a whole-staff CPD session about verbal questioning and using sentence starters in lessons.

- We created a model for facilitating group work and encouraging discussion in all lessons. This included assigning specific roles to students during a group work activity.

- One of the most creative and effective strategies was using props to facilitate oracy across a range of subjects. In performing arts we used a film clapper board, which students held when giving evaluative feedback about a performance, and a megaphone when offering a point for improvement. Each prop had specific sentence starters assigned to them. History used a large mobile phone prop to 'phone a friend' if they were not sure of an answer. Teachers seemed to like this idea, as they could adapt this to their subject or theme.

We did learning walks at the end of the year and the data we collected was encouraging. Verbal sentence starters were being used more regularly in lessons. Teachers had found quizzes to be a fun and accessible way to incorporate oracy and embed vocabulary. Teachers who were interviewed felt more confident about using oracy in their lessons but still felt they had a lot to learn and had only just started to 'scratch the surface' of what is possible.

Ultimately, we concluded that modelling, modelling, modelling was the key for staff (as it is in most teaching!). This included the modelling of presentation and debating skills in lessons, in staff briefings and in the shared spaces around the school. We also showed clips in the whole-staff CPD session of students working within groups, with assigned roles. This seemed to help staff and students enormously. However, the most effective, long-term work took place within curriculum planning. Working with heads of faculties so that oracy informed curriculum content, pedagogy, assessment and feedback methods throughout the school enabled oracy to become embedded over time.

FINDING YOUR BALANCE THROUGH ORACY

Incorporating dialogic teaching into your classroom practice is one of the first steps in ensuring that you have considered and are building on the oracy skills of your learners. By incorporating monologic strategies, you are in essence modelling best practice. However, dialogic teaching strategies are at the heart of deepening the learning process and allowing students to consider more theoretical approaches through the development of logic and contextualisation.

To combine the two approaches, questioning strategies including 'hinge questions' can be used as a doorway that can lead learners into knowledge acquisition. Traditionally referred to as an assessment for learning strategy, these hinge questions act as a formative assessment during a lesson that can allow the teacher to see what students understand. This diagnostic tool can then be used to provide the teacher with an understanding of the level of mastery in the room, enabling the teacher to identify if they can proceed or if they need to readdress a key aspect. Examples of diagnostic tools that could be used include:

- **'traffic light'** system in students' academic journals that can be used to indicate comprehension

    - red = confused and lack of understanding

    - amber = starting to comprehend but more support needed

    - green = understand and confident.

    This is a good starting point to open up discussion and to gauge the level of comprehension of individual students.

- For a quick and easy formative assessment, asking students to indicate their understanding using their hand and a **1–5 scale** is quick, cheap and efficient. It can once again provide an immediate response if the scale is explained and embedded in the practice of the teacher.

- For a more in-depth understanding, **retrieval practice** is an effective tool, not only to judge students' comprehension of a topic, but to allow the teacher to interleave other topics into the questions in order to support knowledge retention. Whether choosing to ask one question or a series of questions, answers will provide a quick understanding of the climate and what areas need further development. Once again, feedback on this can be delivered either in a monologic fashion, based on teacher perception and initial analysis of results, or through dialogic conversation between peers.

Whatever approach you choose to take when it comes to assessing student comprehension, the most important part of any formative assessment is what directly follows the acquisition of information. A common misconception, particularly when practitioners are still new to the classroom, is to see this strategy as more of a 'tick box' exercise as opposed to a diagnostic tool. Their integration of a formative assessment in their lesson structure is there merely to appease the face at the back of the room (it's a 'go to' for lesson observations). However, the assessment on its own would be deemed inappropriate and a complete waste of time. It's what is done as a result of this information that is particularly important to the development of learning. This is where it is useful to be able to acknowledge and identify the strengths of all teaching styles that you have in your toolkit.

If the classroom assessment indicates a lack of understanding, the next steps can be determined by the extension of these issues.

- *Green/High results*

  Continue with the approach that you have intended. However, if this approach is monologic, now would be a good time to encourage peer discussion in order to articulate the learning and explain students' current acquisition.

- *Amber/Medium results*

  These are typically the results that spur a teacher into continuing with their approach in the hope that learning will be embedded more succinctly by the end of the lesson. Once again, allocate time after your whole-class results to promote a discussion between students. Often, issues arise from students' inability to articulate their knowledge, and therefore understanding can be achieved by just recanting the information whilst summarising in their own narrative. This can then be followed with dialogic questioning and a revisiting of the information in order to help students to retain the knowledge through spacing strategies (it would be useful to make a note of the topics and the results of these diagnostics so that you can plan retrieval practice exercises accordingly).

- *Red/Low scoring results*

  Sometimes this can be an issue with comprehension. However, it can also be an issue with confidence. For the class teacher, professional judgement may be necessary to identify the true reason. The key factor is finding the extent of the issue. Once again, allow discussions to support you! Given the time for a reflect and review session with a partner, students will not only feel like they are able to share their confusion or support someone else in finding understanding, but can also ask the question: 'Why?' If students are asked to consider why they have chosen this level of comprehension, they should hopefully be able to indicate their key areas of improvement.

Consequently, it is best to use professional judgement as to how to proceed based on the results that have been acquired. This can mean either continuing with the planned approach or switching the approach in favour of oracy skills and the students' ability to communicate with their peers in order to share and digest the information they have been exposed to. The incorporation of questioning into your lessons needs to be done in a way that considers and utilises the efficiency of dialogic questioning by the teacher, but also involves the encouragement of peer-to-peer conversation in order to embrace students' speaking and listening skills.

Dialogic questioning: developing a deeper comprehension through Socratic talk

In 2017, Tom Sherrington published his book *The Learning Rainforest*, in which he introduced the concept of dialogic questioning in order to develop the understanding and critical thinking of individual students through questioning and further development. His principal idea was to shift specifically towards dialogic questioning in key stage 5, potentially because of the more experienced and focussed cohort, as well as the opportunity that would be given during sessions to explore the rationalisation of individual students.

Most of the research that has been conducted into oracy skills and dialogic strategies appears to focus on primary schools (apart from the research conducted by Voice 21). This is understandable, given the knowledge that the classroom teacher has of a particular cohort in their care. As this cohort remains the same, there is a deeper understanding to be gained regarding the measurement of impact.

This therefore begs the question as to how we can transfer these skills in an environment that is more likely to include a larger group of students who are combined together as a unit, perhaps on a less frequent basis.

Building these dialogic questioning strategies in the secondary classroom involves a lot less of a focus on one-to-one questioning and development than it does at other ages. The high concentration of learners who remain fluid regarding movement means the teacher needs to acquire an immediate interpretation (predominantly through formative assessment and predominantly through closed questioning) quickly in order to understand the learning process in action.

These responses, however, will only give us the surface level understanding of our students. The need to enable students to develop deeper critical thinking is dependent on the next steps and how the learning proceeds. The development of critical thinking to monitor, assess and reflect on one's own knowledge can be seen in the classroom through the efficient use of Socratic questioning techniques.

As Socrates himself once said: 'Questioning is the only defensible form of teaching'. The very premise of learning and development is hinged on the ability to retain and retrieve knowledge, whether this be in the short term, or in the long term through cognitive retrieval.

The use by students of the power of talk and the development of oracy skills in their thinking process not only deepens students' own understanding of subjects, but also enables the teacher to form a summative analysis of the understanding of the cohort as well as their ability to communicate with one another and listen to alternative interpretations. The benefits of adopting strategies such as Socratic questioning lie in the focus placed on the need for the development and expansion of ideas. Embedding this strategy in the classroom will not only enable students to develop confident oracy skills through intellectual dialogue, but will also provide them with a skill that could easily be transferred to their essay writing.

No matter what subject is being taught, the implementation of Socratic questioning, either in a group environment or as a whole-class discussion, can be used to:

1. provide controlled support to the discussions taking place
2. explore more complex ideas in a structured way that allows for visible development
3. analyse and justify concepts in a professional and detailed manner
4. provide an overview of the learning climate
5. identify and challenge any misconceptions.

Socratic questioning can be controlled and developed through a supportive script that can be used either for teacher guidance or as a discussion road map for students in collaborative groups.

The six Socratic questions

The entire premise behind this form of questioning relates to six questions that should be asked in order:

1. clarifying thinking and understanding
2. challenging assumptions
3. probing rationale, reasoning and questioning
4. questioning alternative viewpoints and perspectives
5. reflecting on implications and consequences
6. metacognitive questions.

The appropriate questions to ask can be chosen based on the content, topic and path of the discussion.

Clarifying thinking and understanding	'What exactly does this mean?' 'What is it that you are suggesting? 'What is the question that you are trying to answer?' 'Could you clarify this please?' 'What do we already know about...?' 'Remind me what we already know about...'
Challenging assumptions	'How could you verify or disprove this?' 'What would happen if...?' 'Why do you think this assumption has been made here?' 'Do you agree or disagree with...?' 'Is this always the case?' 'Please explain how/why...'
Probing rationale, reasoning and questioning	'Why would you suggest this?' 'How do you know this to be the case?' 'Can you give me an example of this to support?' 'How might this be refuted?' 'What evidence is there that supports this?' 'Why?'
Questioning alternative viewpoints and perspectives	'What other alternatives could you suggest?' Are there any other viewpoints that you could consider?' 'What might a ____ suggest about this?' 'What is the other side of the argument?' 'Why is your argument the most plausible?' 'What are the strengths and weaknesses of...?'
Reflecting on implications and consequences	'But what would happen if...?' 'How does this affect...?' 'What does our experience tell us?' 'What are the implications of...?' 'How does...fit with what we have learned before? 'Which is the best? Why?'
Metacognitive questioning	'What was so significant about the last question?' 'Why is this question so important? 'What does...mean?' 'What other questions could be asked to deepen our knowledge?'

If you choose to adopt this technique as a teacher, the key is to remember the steps and processes that can be taken to develop the learning of your students through challenge. Don't forget that these techniques should never be reserved specifically for higher ability students. The ability to question our thinking and rationalise our thoughts is a skill that can be demonstrated by everyone no matter what their level of ability is. The only differentiation will be in the answers obtained from these responses.

Sometimes we see this technique being presented as a form of well-scripted theatrical performance, with chairs in circles and different students with different roles. Although this may be a desirable spectacle that, if crafted correctly, could be a beautiful demonstration of the incorporation of oracy in the classroom, we need to be realistic. Incorporating these skills into (where possible) all lessons as opposed to one-off opportunities will consistently allow students to achieve the key requirements of critical thinking. The more they attempt these skills, the less the process will look like some random disco attended by a group of individuals who have no idea how to dance!

The Socratic questioning style is sometimes simplified and redefined in an effort to instil automaticity from students. It is students' own conscious development of thought that will not only lead to them producing deeper and more sophisticated analysis, but will also enable them to provide more captivating and sophisticated conversations (their ability to elaborate on their ideas with adequate justification and developed reasoning as opposed to providing a less riveting conversation through simple sentences and one-word dialogues).

Many have seen this method used in English through the adaptation of the 'What? How? Why?' approach. This approach hinges on the development of one key focus or 'key idea'. From this often simple statement, the process is then elaborated on and developed in a method similar to Socratic questioning. The only difference is that there are fewer stages and the questions themselves are less prescriptive.

What is particularly interesting in this approach is its relation to the outside world and how the knowledge of the three components can actually be reflected in the business world. In order to recognise the significance of this approach, one must first recognise the biological reasoning behind the concept. Whereas the approach commonly adopted in most subjects is to consider the 'What?' first, the economic interpretation questions the necessity to first identify the 'Why?' and then progress in an outside-in model to first distinguish the need before the creation of a product. This approach asks us/students to first consider the elaborate concepts and recognition of human behaviour prior to the channelling of creativity. According to a *Leaderonomics* article by Roshan Thiran:

> Our brain is split into the neo-cortex and the limbic brain. The neo-cortex (how and what) is responsible for all our rational, analytical thought and language. Our limbic brain (why) is responsible for feelings, trust and all human behaviour and decision making with no capacity for language. (Thiran, 2010)

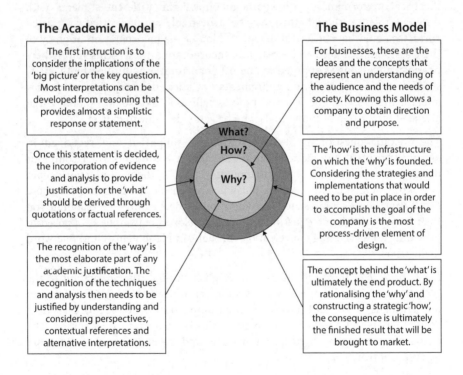

The Academic Model

The first instruction is to consider the implications of the 'big picture' or the key question. Most interpretations can be developed from reasoning that provides almost a simplistic response or statement.

Once this statement is decided, the incorporation of evidence and analysis to provide justification for the 'what' should be derived through quotations or factual references.

The recognition of the 'way' is the most elaborate part of any academic justification. The recognition of the techniques and analysis then needs to be justified by understanding and considering perspectives, contextual references and alternative interpretations.

What?
How?
Why?

The Business Model

For businesses, these are the ideas and the concepts that represent an understanding of the audience and the needs of society. Knowing this allows a company to obtain direction and purpose.

The 'how' is the infrastructure on which the 'why' is founded. Considering the strategies and implementations that would need to be put in place in order to accomplish the goal of the company is the most process-driven element of design.

The concept behind the 'what' is ultimately the end product. By rationalising the 'why' and constructing a strategic 'how', the consequence is ultimately the finished result that will be brought to market.

An alternative interpretation of this approach is the diamond development approach. This was introduced when considering how to support students with their development of reasoning, evaluation, justification and essay construction. The technique can also be used to support interview responses. In a similar manner to when one is being interviewed, it is easy to lose focus and go off on a tangent with responses and ideas, particularly those that build in depth and sophistication.

When introducing students to the diamond development approach (albeit an upside-down model), it is critical that the teacher ensures that the response is allowed to reach a denouement in which the key principle (or the 'what') is revisited in order to revisit the initial statement and further reinforce intellectual interpretation.

The Diamond Development

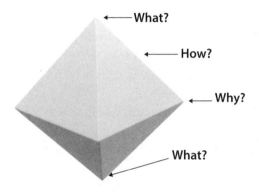

In an interview situation, this technique would be the most logical to ensure that your audience remains captivated and aware of your ability to stay on point. When placed in a situation with very limited think-time or opportunity to construct written support, the ability to recognise the key components of how to answer vital questions that may bring with them a heightened degree of stress is crucial to success.

The benefits of Socratic/deeper questioning include:

✓ the opportunity to encourage student voice in the classroom

✓ a demonstration of the power of open-ended questions

✓ the opportunity to build on and develop active listening skills

✓ the provision of a model of expectation regarding evidence-based arguments

✓ emphasis on the importance of critical reflection

✓ the opportunity to approach real-world problems with the acknowledgement of multiple perspectives

✓ the honing of critical thinking skills in both a subject-specific and a generalised manner

✓ mimicking real-life intellectual discourse to build on skills in the workplace

✓ building oral communication skills with confidence in articulation.

CASE STUDY 9 – ORACY IN DRAMA

In Wales, performing arts specialists like Zak Frost have been working on developing the implementation of oracy assessments through the implementation of a whole-school framework that is used in correlation with those embedded for literacy and numeracy.

The framework is completely coherent with the New Literacy and Numeracy Framework for all Welsh Schools. Prior to creating the Literacy Framework, we followed a generic whole-school policy that was extremely brief. The new Faculty Framework ensures all teaching staff are aware of the expectations for each individual year group. The framework is broken down into three areas: Speaking, Listening and Collaboration and Discussion.

Elements	Aspects	Year 7	Year 8	Year 9
		Learners are able to	Learners are able to	Learners are able to
Developing and presenting information and ideas	Speaking	present topics and ideas clearly, using formal language and varying what they say and how they say it to interest listeners, e.g. expression, tone of voice, volume	present topics and ideas coherently, using techniques effectively, e.g. a clear structure, anecdote to illustrate, plausible conclusions	present ideas and issues convincingly using a range of techniques for impact, e.g. rhetorical questions, appeals to listeners, gestures
		respond to listeners' questions and comments constructively and in detail	respond to listeners' questions and comments constructively and in detail	respond to how listeners are reacting by adapting what they say and how they say it
		argue a convincing case using subject knowledge effectively, e.g. in role or debate	defend a point of view with information and reasons, e.g. in role or debate	sustain a convincing point of view, anticipating and responding to other perspectives, e.g. in role or debate

Elements	Aspects	Year 7	Year 8	Year 9
		Welsh-medium statement: use a range of mutations (soft, nasal and aspirate mutations) correctly in context	Welsh-medium statement: use a range of mutations (soft, nasal and aspirate mutations) correctly in context	Welsh-medium statement: use a range of mutations (soft, nasal and aspirate mutations) correctly in context
	Listening	respond thoughtfully to others' ideas, asking pertinent questions	respond positively and thoughtfully to new ideas and alternative points of view	consider the relevance and significance of information and ideas presented to them
		listen to explanations of processes, sequences or points of view and identify the main points in order	listen to information and ideas (on-screen or live) and identify how evidence is used, e.g. to defend a point of view, or misused, e.g. to mislead by exaggeration	listen to information and ideas and identify how they are presented to promote a particular viewpoint, e.g. use of persuasive language, ignoring inconvenient facts, reaching illogical conclusions
	Collaboration and Discussion	make a range of contributions to discussions, e.g. leading, encouraging and supporting others	take a range of roles, e.g. organising, initiating actions, in more formal group contexts, e.g. when working with unfamiliar peers or adults	take a range of roles in group discussion with greater autonomy, including in more formal situations, e.g. chair, scribe
		reach consensus and agree actions in groups, e.g. agreeing a plan, weighing up reasons and evidence	discuss opposing viewpoints and negotiate ways forward	recognise a range of options for action and reach agreement to achieve the aims of the group

It is vital that we ask students to explain what they know. To achieve this, we need to regularly ask questions of the appropriate type. The following prompts may help during lessons:

- 'Good, can you say that again in a full sentence?'
- 'Can you think of a better phrase for that?'
- 'Explain to me why you think that is true?'
- 'Suppose I was a Y6 pupil, how would you explain that to me?'
- 'You need to tell me at least three different facts about...'
- 'That's right – go on, say a bit more about...'

When the Framework was created, the faculty sat together to look at how each aim could be met in subject areas and what the importance of each aim was. This ensured all staff understood the aims and were able to pick out the key areas of their lessons or scheme of work that would give them the opportunity to meet each aim.

I do not implement the Framework as a 'tick box task'. Students do not have to succeed in every aim or objective. The Framework is there for subject teachers to use as a guide, determine strengths and weaknesses for each individual student and set targets for IDPs. Students have a slightly simplified version in their expressive arts folders and can self-assess and engage in dialogue when developing aims and targets.

POTENTIAL BREAKDOWNS IN COMMUNICATION

10% of conflict is due to difference in opinion. 90% is due to wrong tone of voice

Ritu Ghatourey

Tone of voice

Initially, the concept of tone was one that I was planning to introduce in the chapter that focusses on our volume and pitch. However, understanding and interpreting tone appears more relevant when we consider that a misunderstanding can often result in a breakdown in communication. Firstly, let's consider the different types of tone that we, as practitioners (and communicators!), need to be aware of so that we can identify the most suitable interpretation of a person's tone:

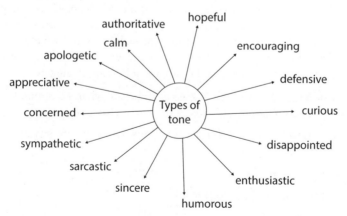

These provide only a miniscule sample from the plethora available when we consider the ability to read and acknowledge an individual's tone of voice.

The vast number of possible interpretations of tone of voice, and the fine line between many tones, will continue to be an issue that students should be made aware of when they are being exposed to oracy skills.

> Tone of voice can convey the emotion behind speech. Strangely, the reasons for voice tone may not be always apparent to the speaker. It may take a careful listener to perceive that someone they are talking to is angry, upset or uncertain. But it is very easy to misinterpret tone of voice, deducing coldness, warmth, impatience, patience, cheerfulness or despair, and so on, when no such quality exists. (Dawes, 2018)

Before exploring the variations between these examples in detail, it is important to recognise that interpreting tone of voice is not to be confused with distinguishing the tone and voice of a piece of writing. Understanding tone of voice derives from the *sound* that is introduced in the spoken word. In academia, we often encourage students to recognise specific tones in transactional writing through linguistic analysis and embedded knowledge. When we consider the tone of voice, we are instead asking them to focus on the phonology of statements and how this can be perceived by the listener(s). When we discuss tone of voice, we are therefore discussing the recognition of rhythm, intonation, volume, pitch and speed.

In educational settings, not only do we need to model the ability to match our tone of voice to our purpose, but we also must ensure that we are supporting students in identifying their own tones and how these may be perceived. In certain circumstances, it may be that the individual is unaware of how they are either demonstrating a negative tone or communicating in a monotonal manner. Often this is the case when teaching students who have been diagnosed with autism and/or have difficulties exhibiting emotions. Dedicating time to the explicit teaching of both recognition and delivery can provide a support strategy that can outlive a student's academic education. When providing explicit instruction, it can be useful to use the following strategies:

- Provide a mood board and discuss examples of when each mood might be exhibited. Relate each of these to a visual cue or 'tell'.

- Discuss how to triangulate interpretations based on a variety of supporting cues:

  - body language
  - the content of the conversation
  - any facial cues
  - the tone of voice.

- Provide examples of tonal fluctuations and extreme interpretations as a register that can support students in gauging the extent of a particular emotion.

When we consider the elements involved in reading a situation, these signals can be a minefield for any intrepid voyager attempting to understand a conversation. This is why we should be constantly and implicitly registering these techniques in the classroom, providing a modelled support in how to implement these skills. Think about when you ask a student a question and they reply with 'I don't know'. What you then must consider is whether you read this statement as a lack of understanding, a fear of making an attempt or a lack of engagement. We can often investigate this in more detail through further subtle questioning and development. When we adopt this technique, students can begin to recognise that a simple 'throwaway' comment can be investigated in more detail to find and address a root cause.

The other examples come from comments such as 'no', 'yes', 'I'm fine' and 'ok', all of which can have a variety of interpretations based on contextualisation.

Along with these foundational knowledge-building strategies, there are other ways that we can have an active discussion in the classroom about how tone can affect our interpretation.

Top tips for engaging with tone of voice:

1. **Active listening.** When students are exposed to a range of approaches and voices, they can then become aware of the effect that these have on learning. Depending on the cohort, they may find the exaggerated and hyperbolic approach tiresome and over the top. Alternatively, they may be disengaged by a lower, more authoritative tone. Finding the balance is crucial, but that doesn't mean it is your responsibility to expose them to a range of tones by yourself! You will find that students are fairly intuitive in reading your emotions after a while. Any deviation that you choose to make could easily come across as disingenuous or hyperbolic.

2. **Collaborative discussions.** The more opportunities that students get to talk to each other the better! The challenge comes when ensuring that these conversations are relevant to learning. In these circumstances, it may be useful to provide a time limit and expectation to support the process.

---

3. **Presentations.** Tone of voice can often affect knowledge retention because of the way that the learning is presented. When one is asked to read aloud – as a teacher or a student – it is easy for one to lose character or volume in one's tone in favour of speed and monotonal presentation. Ask students to investigate a topic or unit and then share this information. Explain to them that this is a project in development. At the start, they can read from a script (but discuss with them how this might affect their delivery). Once this approach becomes embedded, encourage them to deviate from a script and ask them to consider how this has an impact on their presentation. This question can also be asked to an audience to encourage their understanding.

4. **Questioning and expansion.** Challenging tone through questioning allows students to consciously consider the reasons behind the way their information is being presented. If communication lacks intonation, question how they feel about it. If their response comes across as negative, perhaps ask them why. (In these circumstances, it may be that there are indicators of a volatile situation developing. If this is the case, ensure that you are considering how best to diffuse the situation.)

5. **Knowledge is power.** Understanding and articulation are key to being able to confidently address any misconceptions when it comes to dealing with tone of voice. Informing students of an extensive range of examples will not only allow them to recognise specific tones through dialogue, but will also provide them with a subconscious understanding of whatever tone they may be exhibiting.

Accent Discrimination

Unfortunately, accent discrimination, although diminishing in the workplace since the establishment of the Equal Opportunities Commission, is still prevalent in everyday society. If we focus on the perceptions of UK accents in relation to their reception, it is worth looking at how Accent Bias Britain in collaboration with the Queen Mary University of London set out to distinguish any historical and present trends regarding accent discrimination. Their research set out to achieve the following goals:

1. to identify whether accent bias exists in professional hiring contexts and what impacts this can have
2. to understand the cause and effect of any such bias and provide an informed, evidence-based understanding of attitudes to accents in the UK today
3. to test tools, training and techniques that can be used to combat accent bias.

Their research allowed them to compare their acquired data with that collected at other points in time by different researchers investigating the same concept.

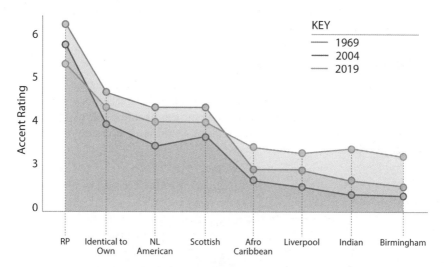

(Accent Bias Britain, 2019)

Despite the encouraging 'levelling' that appears to be occurring and evidence of less explicit bias, there are still critical examples of how judgement and perception are made based on a speaker's origin. Accents such as those from Liverpool or Birmingham are still perceived negatively in terms of their validity and presentation, and stereotypical associations are still made in relation to Afro-Caribbean and Indian accents, thereby showing substantial discrimination.

Accent Bias Britain stated that:

There is some evidence that differences between accents are reducing: while standard accents are still ranked highest and urban and ethnic vernaculars ranked lowest, the quantitative distances between the top-

and bottom-rated accents are smaller in our study than in either 2004 or 1969. Nevertheless, our results show a persistent hierarchy of accent evaluations, one that penalises non-standard working-class and ethnic accents and upholds the belief that national standard varieties are the most prestigious. (Accent Bias Britain, 2019)

While accent discrimination may appear to be out of our control, educators are in a prime position to help ensure that this stereotyping is eliminated. Although the research suggested that differences are declining, there are still elements of a clear hierarchy that need to be eliminated in mainstream education. The opportunity for students to be exposed to speakers with a variety of national and regional dialects will help to promote an inclusive culture that recognises talent and ability over ethnicity or social background.

Adapting to the audience

When we consider the audience exposure of a teacher, it is easy to become overwhelmed by the amount of interaction that takes place on a day-to-day basis with a wide range of recipients. If one were to liken the role to a theatrical one, the different genres and demographics would most certainly overwhelm any scriptwriter.

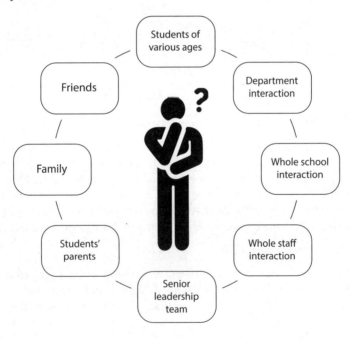

This diagram shows the variety of audience members we must deliver information to on a day-to-day basis, without even including the many other forms of interaction we might engage in, depending on what we have to do on a particular day. Just consider for a moment, then, how we may need to adapt to and differentiate for each of these audiences to convey our intended message.

Some forms of interaction may require a more formal and sophisticated approach, whereas others may require a calm and informal tone that is more welcoming and personal. Consider for a moment whether you have had any experience of mixing up your audience. For example, a partner might comment that you have used your 'teacher tone' in a heated discussion or a request. Or you may have come across as too relaxed and laissez-faire whilst in a professional meeting with management, or used vocabulary that may not have been appropriate. These incidents happen to all of us, and are completely understandable when you consider the persistent demands that we put on our cognitive ability to read, register and respond with an appropriate content and tone for the purpose of each conversation we have.

When we start a dialogue, there are several communication factors we need to consider:

- pitch
- clarity
- tone
- perception and potential reactions
- interpretation.

For communication to be effective and suited to purpose, we need to identify and respond to each of these components, sometimes having to assess the situation very quickly. This is why exposing students to appropriate communication content and audience differentiation through modelling of the correct strategies is so important. When speaking to an audience of any size or demographic, there are also common strategies that need to be either avoided or addressed to achieve success in delivering a message.

Common factors to consider when engaging an audience:

- **Condescending language, tone or visual cues**

  Remember that there is a fine line between simplifying content and appearing demeaning and sarcastic. When talking to staff and students, it is important to recognise that simplification does not imply that you expected the recipient to struggle to comprehend the content, but more likely that you were aware that the recipient could interpret the information in a manner different from that intended. Some recipients may need to repeat information and simplify it for themselves. To the speaker, it may be frustrating or time consuming, but this cannot be reflected in vocalisation or posture.

- **Purpose and intent**

  This focusses more on the root cause of the communication. To open a dialogue, we must first consider its purpose (the learning objective or development intention) and the expected outcome. It is therefore necessary to consider the most suitable audience for the conversation. Consideration of exactly who needs to hear the message allows us to identify the most suitable audience.

- **Complication of content**

  Sometimes less is more. The accelerated learning cycle considers the development of the following key elements: connection of learning to establish knowledge acquisition; activation of learning; demonstration of skills through modelling; and finally a consolidation of skills to ensure retention. In the classroom, these factors are fundamental to ensuring that learning is retained and developed. This approach can also be tailored towards any audience to some extent. Developing familiarity with a topic can support knowledge acquisition through increased confidence and an ability to make informed interpretations. This is then supported by examples, whilst the consolidation comes from dialogic questioning and analysis of summative responses.

- **Vocabulary choice**

  As with content, less is more. It's easy, particularly in circumstances where we need to exhibit an element of professional authority, to become consumed with sophisticated and hyperbolic vocabulary. This can result in a lack of comprehension due to the inability of the recipient to follow the conversation without definitions or expansion. This is similar to the age-old issues that teachers have when exposing students to new and more ambitious levels of vocabulary. If not embedded effectively, the fluidity of the dialogue is halted by either an incorrect interpretation or a lack of understanding.

- **Articulation and formality**

  Articulation is key to clarity. We support comprehension by ensuring that difficulties or misconceptions are dealt with immediately. The level of formality is then suited to the demographic of the audience. While some people see formality as the key to effective behaviour management, it can sometimes come across as intimidating or disconcerting. At the same time, a lack of formality may hinder student judgement around acceptable classroom etiquette. A lot depends on professional judgement in gauging the extent of formality required at any given moment!

- **Interpersonal skills and proximity**

  As previously discussed, physical proximity and an understanding of acceptable distance can play an important role in audience perception and validity. The interpersonal skill involved in understanding this distance helps create a sense of connection with each audience member when speaking to a large group. This can be achieved through:

  - working the room

  - creating an open and active posture

  - maintaining eye contact or at least ensuring that your gaze remains on the audience.

- **Self-awareness over self-depreciation**

  Even when we focus on specific content, we often offer an element of ourselves to the conversation to make our audience (and ourselves) feel at ease. However, we need to do this with care. What can be intended as a strategy that helps us to appear more relatable and 'down to earth' can easily come across as condescending or as evidence of a superiority complex through an acknowledgement of personal accomplishments over content and purpose. At the other extreme, self-deprecation, another common strategy used when presenting to colleagues (in an attempt to be seen as more relatable), can create the impression that we lack validity and are unreliable.

But why do we need to understand our audience?

In 2018, Nadau Klein, working with the University of Chicago, published research into audience perception that determined that is takes milliseconds for an individual to form a judgement of a person. The research involved several case studies using different scenarios, and concluded that a person's perception of their judgement and their actual outcome can be grossly misguided. In teaching terms, consider the use of lesson observations. For a long time, a five- to ten-minute snapshot was seen as an acceptable period in which to make a judgement about a person's overall ability to teach. Although we may have progressed to more holistic methods of assessment, the concept of judgement and immediate perceptions is still a common issue, particularly when dealing with communication.

Klein's studies threw light on this concept:

> In psychology, this is called an empathy gap. Consider the question of how many interactions are necessary for you to decide whether you like and trust someone. It may be tempting to believe you'll rationally evaluate each interaction as you would a dry statistic. But social encounters are vivid and engaging, and the first experience may simply be so absorbing as to tilt your judgment irrevocably, making future interactions unnecessary. (Klein, 2018)

What Klein's study illustrates is the necessity to consider all of the factors identified previously in order to provide a support mechanism for effective communication. Recognising these components and allowing for the opportunity to consider the intended audience could provide the foundations on which to model strong oracy skills with both students and colleagues.

Knowing your audience

When it comes to understanding how your students learn, there are numerous interpretations and approaches that could be adopted. For this particular explanation, I'll be using a strategy that has been adapted based on an understanding of sales and buyer identification.

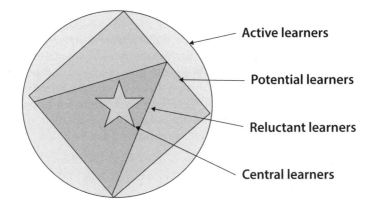

Active learners

Potential learners

Reluctant learners

Central learners

Teachers need to recognise that they teach a classroom of individuals, but if we consider these four different types of learners, it becomes slightly easier to navigate and accommodate the needs of a large cohort of individuals.

Active learners

These are the students who embrace learning and are keen to develop their own subject knowledge. They are the ones keen to interact and demonstrate their skills, whilst considering how they can continue to expand and develop. These students require less explicit teaching and more coaching and guidance to allow them to embark on their own learning journey. Active learners can therefore be summarised as:

✓ Students who constantly engage with and enquire about the content.

✓ Students who thrive off concepts and contextualisation. They are keen to understand the bigger picture.

✓ Students who are keen to consider a broad perception that incorporates numerous factors.

✓ Students who are naturally critical thinkers who question in a positive and inquisitive manner.

✓ Students who require articulation and sophistication. **They thrive on knowledge acquisition and the ability to explore higher-order ideas.**

✓ Students who would prefer to be **guided rather than directed**. They are suited to more independent learning strategies, but will also remain on task throughout collaboration work.

Potential learners

 These students can be slightly more temperamental. They often demonstrate the capability and potential to achieve higher-order thinking, but may not be as independent in their learning. Although they may exhibit comprehension, it is important that these learners are allowed to constantly review and reflect in order to develop their own self-awareness. Potential learners therefore:

✓ May vary in their ability from subject to subject. Ability isn't necessarily natural, but incorporated into engagement and subject-specific capability.

✓ Are capable of achieving critical thinking and subject knowledge, but may lack confidence in their own ability.

✓ Benefit from **positive reassurance** and ownership of abilities.

✓ Can be well structured and articulate in their responses through the incorporation of strategies including the diamond questioning technique and **encouragement of critical thinking**.

✓ Need the space and opportunity to explore their comprehension through collaboration and **supportive communication**. They also benefit from scaffolded foundations on which to expand their own interpretations.

Reluctant learners

 Reluctant learners are more likely to be the minority in the classroom. These are the students who may show deviation from classroom expectations and appear more hesitant in completing tasks. Commonly, this reluctance can be attributed to a lack of comprehension. However, there are often circumstances where other factors need to be taken into consideration. These learners:

✓ May require additional support and a **triangulation** approach with other parties in order to progress. This commonly involves liaising with parents/carers and the pastoral team in order to decide on the most suitable approach.

✓ May appear more defensive, particularly when feeling less able. They can therefore use deviance to mask a lack of comprehension. In these circumstances, guiding them through the learning is important. **Never settle for less** than what you would usually expect, but be prepared to support them in achieving the objective you intended.

✓ Are often the most volatile if approached in the wrong manner. In these cases, it is important to remain calm and in control. Often the key to diffusing a situation is to first be able to **distinguish between the student's emotions and your own** (in some circumstances, this reflection may come after the event, but what is important is that this is considered prior to any restorative justice).

✓ Require constant situational analysis by the practitioner to gauge the best course of action.

Central learners

These students account for most of the class in most circumstances. They are the springboard on which most strategies and approaches will be based. By accounting for the central learners, we can support the implementation of monologic and dialogic approaches to knowledge acquisition based on our knowledge of the cohort. When approaching central learners, we need to:

✓ Consider them as the key demographic that will support the initial strategies that we can adopt for the various learning objectives.

✓ Consider, in relation to teacher-led strategies, that this cohort will benefit from the continual use of the **accelerated learning cycle** alongside consistent use of scaffolding, questioning and modelling in order to demonstrate what is expected of students.

✓ Consider that these students will also benefit from **peer collaboration** and discussion-based approaches in order to encourage more independent reflection and self-confidence in their subject knowledge.

Interestingly, developing comprehension of these different strategies can also be relevant when embarking on leadership-based roles.

Active	Those colleagues who are keen to explore their own professional development strategies. They always want to expand on their skills and are supportive in embracing the whole-school ethos.
Potential	Colleagues who have demonstrated that they are extremely capable and a specialist in their field. They may not be as 'hands on' when introducing initiatives or approaches, but they are able to adopt these strategies successfully when they present a 'buy in' mindset.
Central	Those who can complete their job description and do so to the best of their ability. These colleagues may not show a desire to progress professionally, but that does not mean that they should be disregarded. These are the colleagues that are central to the efficient running of the school.
Reluctant	These colleagues may prove slightly trickier to get engaged with any new strategies or approaches, particularly new ways of working. They are not necessarily defensive, but may require more support and explanation to develop their comprehension and reasoning.

Top tips for avoiding communication breakdowns

1. Preparation is key

 You know what they say, 'failing to prepare is preparing to fail'. We've all been in situations (whether out of our control or not) where we have had to either go off script or break into an impromptu monologue. In these circumstances, it is easy to lose focus and therefore lose the comprehension of an audience. These situations can sometimes be unavoidable and shouldn't be feared. However, they can be counteracted by having most of our professional communications more scripted and prepared.

Each scenario and audience may call for a different approach to preparation; it's completely dependent on how one plans and what works best.

- In lessons, preparation is often the planning of the lesson considering the objectives and intended outcomes of the session/ learning.

- In meetings or training where you are presenting, this could be more scripted and note-based.

- Even in interviews, this could be a consideration of the high-frequency questions and how best to respond to them.

Ultimately, preparation for dialogue will allow you to appear more confident and articulate. It will ensure that all of your key points are covered, whilst providing a framework which allows you to cope with potential alterations or adaptations that may need to be made in the moment.

2. Read the signals

Unfortunately, when dealing with larger audiences, there will be an array of opportunities to read perhaps more disconcerting examples of visual cues. Reading the signals doesn't necessarily require the ability to provide a psychoanalytic interpretation of each individual's mannerisms. However, in small audiences and one-to-one scenarios, reading the signals is relevant. The ability to read the signals of communication derives from the recognition of the key components of oracy skills.

- Physical cues

    - Are they showing an open posture and agreeable signals (head nodding, smiling, hand gestures)?

    - Are they closed and more introverted in their body language?

    - What does their facial expression suggest (Confusion? Agreement? Distraction?)

- Linguistic cues

    - Does their vocabulary choice during interaction imply positive interaction?

    - Are they utilising or responding to any rhetorical techniques?

    - Do their responses and dialogue indicate a cognitive comprehension of the content?

- Social and emotional

    - Has the conversation implications on the zone of proximity?

    - Has the recipient reacted in the way intended?

    - Is the recipient able to acknowledge comprehension through listening and responding where appropriate?

3. Feedback develops the foundations

 We can't shy away from feedback. While some may attempt to shy away from positive comments, others fail to differentiate emotionally from any negative feedback they may receive. In any circumstance, it is feedback and reflection that drives development in all aspects of learning and professional development. The acquisition of feedback is another one of those circumstances that is predominantly based on situational analysis. The most suitable approach is dependent on the number of recipients and the detail of feedback that is required. By factoring in these considerations, one is then able to decide on the most effective strategy to proceed with:

- larger audiences
- smaller audiences
- one-to-one conversation.

Approaching verbal feedback with students

When the EEF summarised the effectiveness of providing feedback to learners about their improvement and how they can make progress, they surmised that the results, when this is done properly, can amount to additional progress of eight months. When this was first published, the ultimate perception was to stoke the marking engine with high (and sometimes unrealistic) expectations. When considering feedback, marking is only one aspect, however, with the EEF actually specifying that verbal feedback has the potential to have just the same impact as marking. The prominent difference is that the incorporation of verbal feedback into everyday practice can have a substantial positive impact on efficiency and speed (thus supporting teacher workload).

Working on our ability to provide verbal feedback can allow feedback to be done more frequently and thus creates a wider scope for development.

In 2019, Ross McGill, alongside University College London, researched and published a framework based on the implementation of verbal feedback in the classroom. In this research, the goal was to embark on evidence and strategies that could:

- dramatically reduce the quantity of written feedback and, instead, provide instant verbal feedback in lessons

- develop an ethos in which teachers can focus on the learning of the pupils
- create an environment where teachers can dedicate their working time to developing technological feedback strategies
- foster targeted talk about knowledge and skills
- encourage pupils to think about where they're going, how well they are getting on and what's next.

McGill, 2019

The research and recommendations considered strategies that could easily be adopted in the classroom:

ABC	As previously discussed, this approach encourages fluidity of dialogue by asking students to either agree, build on, or challenge a statement.
Cold-calling	A 'no hands up' technique that allows the teacher to gauge feedback from specific students in the classroom.
C3B4Me	Asking students to consider alternative sources of help before the teacher is a technique used to support resilience, capability for more self-reflection, and self-assessment strategies.
DIRT	Dedicated improvement and reflection time is the time allowed to develop work based on feedback provided. Whether written or verbal, the ability to act on this is crucial to developing subject capabilities.

Although there was no specific prescriptive response for all schools to develop their ability to deliver verbal feedback, there was a clear perception that the use of this strategy can actually serve the same purpose as written marking.

Verbal feedback, when applied well, has a positive impact on the engagement of all students (including those who are disadvantaged). It may also lead to gains in progress and achievement and – at the least – appears to have no detrimental effects. When teachers learn to apply verbal feedback strategies consistently and with confidence it has a marked positive effect on their overall practice and on the time they have available for other teaching tasks such as planning. (Quinn, 2019)

The teachers involved in the process identified features of the practice that benefitted the staff in some way:

- 61% found that their lesson planning improved with more time being available and the focus being specifically on the needs of the students.

- 30% deduced that the approach made them more confident, as they were willing to engage in further research and were not concerned by the marking workload.

- 77% identified a distinct reduction in workload, with less time being spent marking.

It is clear that by supporting teachers in the development of a culture that is keen to embrace verbal feedback as an approach to facilitating learning we not only consider the efficiency of oracy skills in improving the lives of our students, but also utilise the same skills to include other positive contributions to education and practice.

Approaching verbal feedback with staff

One of the most effective methods of reflection that can contribute to an informed and detailed discussion on feedback is a reflection scale. This can often be used as a tool to guide, support and evaluate communication. Providing a strategy that can be used prior to a discussion can be particularly useful in conversations regarding professional development or lesson/termly focus. The technique is simple. The aim is to use an arrow to position key elements on a sliding scale, depending on where they might fit. These key elements could be the teaching standards or components of a particular lesson. But what they do is enhance the focus of feedback more towards the recipient's capacity to reflect rather than towards the observer's or coach's ability to 'diagnose'.

DEVELOPING ORACY IN LEADERSHIP

At the heart of effective leadership is the ability to communicate with a variety of audiences. Only by liaising with and instilling our knowledge and requirements in others can we demonstrate our ability to lead successfully. Whether you are leading a cohort of peers or you are leading in the classroom, recognising the skills and techniques that can be used to support your message delivery can, in essence, play a substantial role in achieving your goal.

When we think about the necessity to be an effective communicator in order to lead, we need to acknowledge that there are a number of different forms that can fall underneath this umbrella. Methods of communication that we might take into consideration when introducing strategies include:

- an informal dialogue between two people
- a formal meeting
- addressing a larger cohort (a group of colleagues or a class of students)
- written forms of communication.

In 2016, *Forbes* magazine published an article that looked specifically at the traits of effective leadership through communication. The article specified that:

As a leader, great communication is critical not just to provide details about the mission and vision of what you are trying to accomplish, but also to motivate, inspire and manage relationships to move people in a desired direction.

When in a leadership position, we often don't realize that the spotlight is always on us. Everything we say and do is being scrutinized, for better or for worse. By accepting both the honor and challenge of leading a team, it is important to remember that what we do both on and off the 'battlefield' [a]ffects our ability to lead. Words and actions can become habits and habits contribute to defining our character. Leadership is a privilege that must be earned every day. (Gleeson, 2016)

The purpose of the article was to outline the key traits that are required to successfully lead and communicate with others. The five key factors can therefore be acknowledged and transferred to a variety of education-based environments; whether you are delivering a session to peers or teaching in the classroom, these can remain the same no matter what the environment.

Be present

Distraction is obvious. When we are not 100% focussed on what is right in front of us, it becomes apparent to the audience. A lack of engagement with the subject matter results in a strained dialogue between you and the recipient. It is therefore important that you show your ability to focus on what is there and occurring in the present moment. By giving the matter your full attention, you are more likely to support the development of a rapport between yourself and the recipient. If your own interest is not communicated by you or received by the other party, this could consequently lead to hostility or a lack of enthusiasm for the topic of conversation.

In a classroom, this could mean that students perceive your content as lacking interest or validity. They could also begin to disengage with learning and consequently either become disruptive or participate in behaviour that deviates from expectations.

In management, it can suggest to staff that their interaction is inadequate or inconvenient. Although true perceptions are obviously subject to individual interpretation, the lack of engagement with recipients does result in less of an open and approachable leadership style.

Tips to support

- If necessary, ask the person who wants to communicate to wait a few seconds so that you can finish the task that may distract you. Just as we ask students to finish what they're doing, we need to make sure that we have achieved our own denouement before embarking on any conversations.

- When dealing with deviant behaviour, keeping your focus specifically on the delivery of dialogue can be achieved through simple gestures and body language recognition.

- If needs be, schedule appointments for students or staff so that you can set aside designated time where you are unlikely to be disturbed (unless in the case of an emergency).

> • If needs be, move away from anything that may distract you from listening. For example, you may want to move away from any devices that might draw your attention away from the present.

Ask the right questions

Leadership doesn't have to be about owning the room or being the smartest person in it! Asking the right questions can lead to the fostering of productive and intelligent communication in which you act as the facilitator to encourage collaborative questioning and development as a cohort. This entails avoiding a more dictatorial approach in the shape of posing questions instead of providing answers. By guiding such conversations, students can gain a deeper independent understanding of concepts and staff can claim ownership in strategic development and evaluation.

> *Tips to support*
>
> • Ensure that questions are open and allow for ideas to be expanded on through simple deepening.
>
> • It could be useful to consider your questions prior to the conversation or lesson. This means that the questions can be adapted where necessary and that the adequate foundations are in place to ensure that learning/training approaches are developed.
>
> • Acknowledge the fact that, when dealing with colleagues, you will not be the expert on every single subject and every element of pedagogical knowledge. Effective leadership requires knowledge of and delegation based on the strengths of your staff in order to achieve the highest potential possible.

Speak less, listen more

We're all guilty of at some point exhibiting poor listening skills. Although we may not be consciously making the decision to disengage with the dialogue, it is quite common to be thinking more about what we are going to say next as opposed to listening to what is being spoken. Keen on considering what we are going to say, we then become guilty of poor listening skills that inhibit our ability to effectively communicate.

177

As with the previous factor, high calibre leadership is all about developing dialogue with others rather than leading a one-sided perception and approach. Admittedly, as with the recognition that both dialogic and monologic teaching are both useful approaches to teaching in the classroom, there will always be circumstances where there is a distinct need for clarity and explicit instruction. In these cases, it is vital that the information is given clearly and with minimal exaggeration or hyperbole. In essence, keep it simple and straight to the point, and then allow time to listen to thoughts and opinions.

Tips to support

- Consider what approach is best suited to the information that you are trying to convey to your audience. Once this is planned, ensure that all information is clear and concise.

- It may be useful to provide visual support in order to develop knowledge acquisition and deliver the key information.

Consider your emotional intelligence

Considering and interpreting any emotional content of communication should not be perceived as simply a 'soft' leadership approach. Rather, it is the ability to recognise characteristics and be competent with understanding your audience, and is technically what we could also refer to as the ability to read a room.

Much of this has to do with the previously acknowledged components of effective oracy skills – being both empathetic and self-aware. It is the ability to recognise a situation and emotion based on elements such as body language, tone and pace of speech. Reading your recipient's emotions through assessing their speech should support your ability to adapt and strategically guide your responses in order to avoid negative repercussions.

In class, this can be exemplified by considering the effect of pushing a student outside of their comfort zone. In these circumstances, it is important to be able to recognise the difference between a positive stressor and a negative one. If a student feels uncomfortable, their posture and tone may change, and they may become withdrawn and inaudible. If the situation is read incorrectly and pushed further, this could potentially lead to negative behaviour and a volatile encounter.

When considering colleagues, this factor involves the ability to think about whether or not a conversation is relevant or necessary at a particular moment in time. If a colleague is displaying signs of agitation and stress, it would be unwise to enter into a conversation in that moment that may add to the situation (this is, of course, unless it is necessary to do so). Often, recognising that it would be wiser to approach a subject at a calmer time may lead to a calmer and more composed conversation that allows for reflection and realism to play a part in the outcome.

Keep calm and carry on

Panic is never a positive. There is a distinct difference between stress and panic; stress is a heightened emotion that provides for a rapid response to alleviate the issue, whereas panic is an immediate and exaggerated reaction to a situation. Panic is, of course, contagious, and should be eradicated (or at least lessened) before one speaks.

Often, this is a response of a mind wanting to provide an immediate reaction to a stressor. This results in words being said or decisions being made that on reflection are unnecessary. It is easy for individuals to subconsciously mirror our body language and communication. If we become confrontational, chances are that they will too. If we are dealing with a heightened situation and we demonstrate a calm and collected manner, it is likely that this will support students in reducing their negative attitude.

This is not to say that the key to success is the ability to not become stressed and retain a cool, calm demeanour at all times. In some circumstances, it is important to remind staff about the analogy of a fizzy drink bottle. The more that the bottle is shaken, the more compressed the gas. If the bottle is continuously shaken with the lid tightened, it is likely that the bottle will explode as a result of the inability of the bottle to contain the pressure. If the lid is gently unscrewed so that air can slowly be released, the gradual release in air pressure will prevent an explosion from taking place.

Navigating written communication

Mehrabian (1972) is often commonly misquoted for his research into body language. Amongst those who consider styles of communication important, it's implied that 93% of all communication is non-verbal. If this were the case, I would predict a lot more of us would dare to include an emoji in our professional correspondence. The realistic conclusion when considering communication is that although 7% of comprehension comes from the words used, 38% of inference is derived from the tone of voice, volume, rate of speech and pitch, and 55% is from facial expressions, hand gestures, postures and other forms of body language. The overarching statement when acknowledging these nuggets of knowledge would be that we rely on a combination of factors to get our desired message across as accurately as possible.

So, what do we do when some key points of communication are taken away? How do we support circumstances where our only form of communication may not necessarily be face to face? Although this may not be oracy specific, the ability to identify and master the skill of all types of communication is what will allow for efficiency of communication. When there are moments when visual cues aren't necessarily available, there are certain tips that could help to prevent any misunderstandings.

Start off small

The tone of emails can always be judged by their signature. Trawl through your emails and you will soon discover that, no matter how diligent you are, you appear to have a specific 'tell' based on your audience and the subject matter. Upon doing this little reflection myself, I began to recognise certain key traits:

1. *Thanks* – General email to a member of the department. Non-judgemental and straight to the point.

2. *Thanks in advance* – One of those situations where the task you've set is almost expected (whether the recipient likes it or not).

3. *Kind regards* – Usually to a parent or a senior professional who you are aware probably doesn't know your name and to whom you'd be inclined to curtsey if you were to ever meet them.

4. *Regards* – A less attached signature that could quite easily be saved for those letters or emails that you're writing against your will.

5. *Nothing* – Straight to the point, almost an air of 'no time for chit chat, get the job done'. This is the easiest to be misconstrued depending on the audience and the topic.

But what if these traits became a bit disjointed in times such as our current pandemic??

What if you went to complete the email, and then realised that the baby was on a one-person mission to attack the dog? Or that the eldest had taken what he'd learnt about volcanoes and was attempting to create an experiment in the kitchen sink?

All of a sudden, we lose focus. We become distracted and perplexed to the point that our professional tone goes out of the window.

All of a sudden, we're less of the suit-wearing professional, and more like a sweatpants-wearing circus act with so many plates in the air that we're recreating a Greek restaurant dance act!

The point is that one of the main areas that people need to consider during this unprecedented time is the way that emails are being constructed. The very consideration of this fact will (hopefully) lead you down the righteous path of effective communication.

What is the solution?

Interpreting the content of communication is quite simple really, but can easily be misunderstood. Nobody should be over-analysing their correspondence. The last thing that should happen is that you begin to expand your CPD through the psychoanalysis of every single lexical choice you've made.

Your request for a new password doesn't have to sound like an extract of Dickensian gratuity. There are, however, simple tricks that can at least begin to support your approach.

- Proofread your email! How many times is this yelled at students on a daily basis in schools up and down the country? Why do we think that we are any better? If anything, could our age, experience and knowledge actually make us more complacent?

- Think about clarity. Are you getting your point across? If you're asking a question, it shouldn't be a two-page essay. At the same time, if you're discussing a sensitive matter, then two simple sentences aren't really going to cut it.

- Consider your audience. When all else fails, keep it formal and keep it simple. If you're testing the waters to check Fred's 'toilet humour level', then doing it at a time where you can't gauge his facial response or reaction might not be advisable.

- Think about whether a video call would be the more beneficial option if a face-to-face meeting would be impractical.

Obviously, there will always be moments where our attempts to be in tune with our communication skills will land us flat on our face. What matters most is what we take from these moments and how we move forward, instead of creating a domino effect of misinterpretation and miscommunication.

Reading face-to-face conversations

What are the most daunting words to hear from a colleague, student, friend or family member?

'I'm fine.'

In a normal day-to-day conversation, this simple statement could be a throwaway response to a simplified enquiry into a person's health. Now consider this statement of a leader. Whether in the context of guiding a group of students or coaching a cohort of colleagues, the phrase can easily be perceived as a misdirection or a warning sign of difficulties that could potentially arise. In these circumstances, we need to consider how we perceive the statement itself. What are the signals we can use to determine a true feeling or emotion?

Think about their body language – Are they busying themselves and avoiding eye contact? Are their movements perhaps more animated and progressively louder?

Think about their tone – Does the response appear rehearsed? Is there a reassurance visible or is it more like an avoidance?

Contextualise the situation – How would you react in a similar circumstance? What has actually happened and how might that make a person feel? What are the realistic emotions that one might demonstrate in these situations?

In any circumstances, the ability to understand the situation without necessarily provoking a conflict is a substantial step forward in the effort to develop a strong and connected team of individuals. By taking into consideration the same visual cues that we teach our students, we can build on our own capacity to master oracy skills.

Teacher coaching

There are several reasons why promoting coaching within your educational setting can contribute to the professional development and communication of colleagues.

- Coaching models can support in the planning and implementation of effective coaching. These therefore provide a consistent framework for the flow of conversation.

- Coaching interaction allows staff members to communicate with each other and provides opportunities to collaborate with colleagues with whom they may have little interaction.

- This approach works to improve the environment by focussing on the development of each of the staff members. Instead of attempting to deal with situations as and when they arise, it instead seeks to develop foundations and consequently improves the long-term successes of the setting.

Coaching models

The embedding of a coaching model in schools has become more routine across schools that are keen to support their staff and encourage professional development throughout the school. The purpose of the implementations of coaching models is therefore to support an individual through the following steps:

1. Understanding where an individual is currently at in their career.

2. Exploring the options available to the individual (including career development and progression).

3. Establishing a desired goal that the individual would like to achieve.

4. Determining any obstacles and what can be done to avoid or negotiate these.

5. Creating a plan of action with SMART targets (specific/measurable/ achievable/relevant/time-based).

As with most pedagogical approaches, there are quite a number of models that can be adopted when implementing a coaching strategy. The models may have different acronyms and approaches, but they are all founded on the key intention of providing a supportive dialogue that can be adapted to establish a goal, consider opportunities and establish an action plan to encourage implementation.

Of all the acronyms available, the most common approach is the GROW model.

G	Goal	Establishing the goals and intentions supports the idea of this being a purposeful conversation. The recognition of an individual's goals will help in guiding the rest of the conversation.
R	Reality	This is about encouraging reflection and evaluation of the current position, and therefore explores the individual's current position relating to their goal. It also allows for an opportunity to explore strengths and weaknesses in more detail.
O	Options	Options is the focus on potential opportunities that could be explored to encourage an active move towards achieving goals. By considering all options available and possible routes, the subject is well informed before implementing a specific timeline.
W	Wrap up	Before bringing the conversation to the close, it is important to establish any next steps and SMART targets that can guide the individual towards reaching their goal.

In order to ensure that this dialogue is purposeful and meaningful, it is useful for participants to have a supportive script similar to those that we would provide to students to ensure that we maintain a focussed outcome from the conversation.

Goal

✓ What do you want to achieve from this coaching session?

✓ What goal do you want to achieve?

✓ What would you like to happen with _____?

✓ What do you *really* want?

✓ What would you like to accomplish?

✓ What result are you trying to achieve?

✓ What outcome would be ideal?

What do you want to change?

✓ *Why* are you hoping to achieve this goal?

Reality

✓ What is happening now (what, who, when, and how often)? What is the effect or result of this?

✓ Have you already taken any steps towards your goal?

✓ How would you describe what you did?

✓ Where are you now in relation to your goal?

✓ On a scale of one to ten, where are you?

✓ What has contributed to your success so far?

✓ What progress have you made so far?

✓ What is working well right now?

✓ What is required of you?

✓ Do you know other people who have achieved that goal?

✓ What did you learn from _____?

✓ What have you already tried?

✓ How could you turn this around this time?

✓ What could you do better this time?

✓ If you asked _____, what would they say about you?

Options

✓ What are your options?

✓ What do you think you need to do next?

✓ What could be your first step?

✓ What do you think you need to do to get a better result (or closer to your goal)?

✓ What else could you do?

✓ Who else might be able to help?

✓ What has worked for you already? How could you do more of that?

✓ What is the hardest/most challenging part of that for you?

✓ What advice would you give to a friend about that?

✓ What would you gain/lose by doing/saying that?

✓ What's the best/worst thing about that option?

✓ Which option do you feel ready to act on?

✓ What could you do differently?

✓ Who do you know who has encountered a similar situation?

✓ If anything were possible, what would you do?

Wrap up

✓ How are going to go about it?

✓ What do you think you need to do right now?

✓ Tell me how you're going to do that.

✓ How will you know when you have done it?

✓ Is there anything else you can do?

✓ On a scale of one to ten, what is the likelihood of your plan succeeding?

✓ What would it take to make it a ten?

✓ What obstacles are getting in the way of success?

✓ What roadblocks do you expect or will require planning?

✓ What resources can help you?

✓ Is there anything missing?

✓ What is one small step you can take now?

✓ When are you going to start?

✓ How will you know you have been successful?

✓ What support do you need to get that done?

Triangulation

Triangulation is another form of coaching, but this approach can be less prescriptive and more of a dialogue as opposed to a specific outcome. The principle behind triangulation is the ability to allow staff to collaborate with others across the setting whilst taking into consideration the strengths and weaknesses of each individual. The effectiveness of this approach is dependent on the implementation of a pedagogical audit prior to groups being confirmed. Establishing capabilities first ensures the effectiveness of these collaborative groups.

Although the common purpose of triangulation is the introduction of a mediator into a dialogue that may require a third party to interject and advise where necessary, coaching triangulation provides different advice perspectives that should result in a more informed discussion and consideration of techniques.

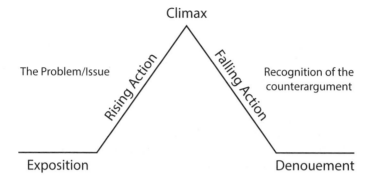

The reason that these groups are less scripted is to encourage staff to participate in more open channels of communication in order to develop their own practice without labelling it as a specific requirement or a 'top down' expectation. The aim of providing groups with a specific focus point is to encourage them to approach the component in the way that suits them best. It could be that they choose to participate in action research and theoretical understanding of the concept. Alternatively, this could provoke them to share specific classroom approaches and to reflect on these appropriately.

Top tips for effective leadership communication (summary)

- Daily (or even weekly) check-ins with members of staff or students can help to identify any situations before they develop into a serious issue.

- Recognise that each individual may demonstrate different reactions or different indicators that will support your interpretation of how they're feeling. It is your responsibility to know your team as individuals as opposed to a cohort.

- Think about the factors that can affect the outcome of a conversation. It is important to consider the contributing factors such as time, location and form before you initiate certain types of discussions.

  - It might be that you may need to schedule a formal meeting.

- Remember that breaks or dinner times are scarce and sacred, so having a meeting at those times defies the purpose of their existence.

- There are those who may dwell on the content of a meeting if you schedule one in advance. Make sure that you provide a brief summary of the purpose so that, if necessary, the individual has time to prepare.

- Remember that communication can't all be a one-way street. Effective leaders are those who acknowledge that they may not have the answers or the knowledge for everything. They instead respect the specialism of those around them and encourage collaboration and progressive coaching.

- Ensure that communication is meaningful and that the intention is achieved. Sometimes this may mean that the conversation needs to be summarised to establish specific points of significance.

- Development from communication is not linear regarding positions. Often it is the encouragement of peers in a realistic and truthful discussion that can provide the most effective outcome for an individual.

CASE STUDY 10 –
INTRODUCING ORACY
THROUGH LEADERSHIP

Helen Mars holds a teaching and learning role in a high-achieving state grammar school in the north of England, and has been working with the literacy coordinator/head librarian to push the implementation and effective use of oracy in her setting.

Having already covered Tier 2 vocabulary in whole-staff training and in weekly updates via the incorporation of 'word' and 'poem' of the week, I felt strongly that authenticity and purpose needed to be at the forefront of my campaign to counteract any potential pushback from staff or pupils who may see oracy as an optional extra and not helpful in securing top grades or university places.

To staff in a training day, I launched the focus with a very personal and impassioned explanation of the obstacles and potential that I had gained from oracy and literacy as a working-class teenager. I gave the staff a crash course in language terminology, such as accent, dialect, sociolect, hedging, fillers and code switching, and did work in department groups to unpick potential bias, assumptions and pitfalls teachers might have when teaching or correcting language.

Again, the clear message was that we are all teachers of oracy in all lessons, and staff in all subjects needed the confidence to correct and stretch spoken language.

I also highlighted ways to embed and scaffold oracy tasks in lessons, giving out ready-made resources like planning sheets and peer feedback guidance, so staff could start using it the very next day: otherwise I always think that well-meaning but busy teachers don't get a chance to use new ideas, and then they are lost in the churn of term.

Repeatedly stressing the workload implications of spoken tasks was popular too: that teacher marking could be reduced at pinch points in term, such as when marking year 11 mocks. This got more ambivalent teachers sitting up and listening. What was also helpful was showing a range of tasks, like balloon debate, role play and mock trials, and not just presentations.

Coupled with the push on empowering teachers, I also held high-profile events in and outside school such as English-Speaking Union competitions. A colleague ran a weekly informal debate club. House debate is the next step, sadly curtailed this year with coronavirus closure. The school already has events where oracy is valued, and again a next step is to ensure this is highlighted and used more effectively where possible. Year 9, for example, have a drop-down day at a local National Trust site to learn about marketing and team work, and year 8 have a three-day engineering and architecture group task which culminates in presentations, and again there's scope for more emphasis on the quality of their speaking overall.

We also have a number of visiting authors and speakers in the year, and I hope to train up students to be better at asking questions and making useful comments in question and answer sessions. With a large number applying to Oxbridge each year, I want to do more work on preparing all students for interviews, not just in terms of smart suits and handshakes, but explicitly teaching to students' techniques for logical explanations and debate.

THE ART OF DEBATE

Don't raise your voice, improve your argument.
> Desmond Tutu [Address at the Nelson Mandela Foundation in
> Houghton, Johannesburg, South Africa, 23 November 2004]

The implementation of debate in the classroom has been an effective and efficient strategy for improving oracy skills in academia. Students' ability to articulate a solid response under pressure is a sure indication of a school that has nurtured and developed spoken language and critical thinking skills.

Reasons for debate

By the very act of arguing, you awake the patient's reason; and once it is awake, who can foresee the result?
> C.S. Lewis

There are several explanations as to why incorporating debate strategies, or even the creation of a debate club in your school, could act as a catalyst for learning and development. These positive factors include, but are not limited to:

- The ability to promote the formation of opinions that are focussed specifically on the views and opinions of the individual, but in a rational and considerate manner.

- Explaining the significance of justification and the need to provide evidence to support the validity of any statements.

- The development of collaborative skills to work with other members of the group as well as against peers. This includes the ability to counter any ideas without coming across as short or abrasive.

- The potential to gain an insight into parliamentary debates and how they are used to make critical decisions that affect all members of society.

- The acknowledgement of a variety of viewpoints and perspectives and how these can be questioned or discussed in a safe environment that promotes focussed communication and debate.

The key components of debating skills are the ability to be part of an active discussion and to engage in dialogue that is centred around a specific topic or statement. In English Language, this is often associated with any questions that focus on the skill of critical evaluation or the ability to demonstrate different viewpoints or perspectives through a piece of transactional writing.

By incorporating these strategies into the classroom, the teacher can maintain a facilitator role within the learning environment whilst maintaining clear control of the classroom. The ability to conduct a debate can be likened to the ability to conduct an orchestra. The unification of various instruments, playing at different volumes, with different tones and sounds, needs to be supported so that the outcome is more classical music than chaos.

The important thing to recognise is that this does not require silence. Volume is a good thing; hearing an intellectual dialogue taking place in the classroom is one of the most rewarding elements that a teacher can experience. This can be achieved in any setting if the teacher lays clear expectations and there is a collective understanding of what is required.

Introducing debate in the classroom

The best place to start with any form of debate is to first focus on the listening skills that are required for a debate to proceed. It is often quite easy for teenagers to formulate an opinion on a subject. Through any monologic teaching that takes place in the classroom, listening skills should be embedded into the commonplace expectations of the classroom. A key way of reinforcing the automaticity of this skill would be to first define the concept of debate in its entirety. The facilitation of a discussion around the definition of debate needs to end in an understanding that there are three key aspects to a successful debate:

- listening to others and responding accordingly

- speaking clearly and audibly to ensure comprehension

- justification of ideas through reasoned development.

Once the students have begun to appreciate the acknowledgment of these key components and how they are integral to effective debating, you may find that it is easier to introduce effective strategies that are more likely to be embedded over time.

Approaching debate in the classroom

1. Encourage the ability to **define** a debate.
2. Lay out clear **rules and expectations** that will support and encourage the participation of all.
3. Consider topic points that will allow for the beginnings of **generalised discussion** in the classroom (this could potentially be scaffolded and supported through the incorporation of ABC questioning).
4. **Preparation** is key! Promote more developed and well researched pieces, whether through collaboration or as an individual.

Encourage the ability to define a debate.

Listening is particularly important when students begin to recognise that the most effective debates need to include an active dialogue. This dialogue needs to be developed and formulated through research and preparation, but also through reactive responses based on the information provided by one's opponent.

The concept of debate needs to be interpreted as fluid and interchangeable as opposed to stagnant and clear-cut. By learning how to listen and adapt, students gain knowledge of an integral life skill that they will need to utilise in later life. Whether they are caught up in a discussion with their peers or their professional career requires them to rationalise and consider viewpoints from different parties, the ability to listen is the core foundation of effective speaking and listening. This appreciation of listening therefore not only promotes the incorporation of reactive dialogue, but also supports the development of power and knowledge.

Lay out clear rules and expectations that will support and encourage participation of all.

As with all incorporation of spoken language in the classroom, there needs to be a clear understanding of expectations and acceptable behaviour. To support the development of a calm and organised climate for debate, providing tailored topic points that will provoke a clear response can often be instrumental in laying the foundations of communication. The more confident a student feels about the subject that is being discussed, the more likely they are to contribute in some form. Once this foundation is achieved, it is important to expose students to a variety of topics and focus points. The desire to venture down the avenue of engagement can actually have a detrimental effect on learners, as it hinders their exposure to topics through fear, and they may be foreign or negatively received.

The handling of and reaction to any perspectives or viewpoints that may provoke an emotional response is a crucial part of dealing with debate. As the activity may cover particularly sensitive subjects, it is vital that students are provided with an understanding of acceptance and tolerance. By considering different opinions or thoughts, students can approach these sessions in a manner that promotes equality and diversity.

Consider topic points that will allow for the beginnings of generalised discussion in the classroom.

Formulating effective debate strategies requires the ability to reason with or present a perspective on a variety of topics. These topics are often enticing, with their specific social, moral or spiritual focus points. A good place to begin embedding debating skills is through PSHE lessons, allowing students to gain a deeper understanding of their own beliefs and interpretations whilst promoting the sharing of these perspectives in a calm and reasoned manner.

When considering implementing a debate approach to introduce a specific topic or focus point (in any subject), one must first consider the type of debate topic that is being introduced. Understanding each of these allows us to present reasonable topic focus points in our relevant subject.

Motions of fact

These are the factual interpretations of a certain question, meaning that the focus is on whether a statement can be perceived as true or not.

Examples:

- Limiting drug availability is the most effective way of limiting the impact of drugs in society.
- Which has the biggest influence on our development, nature or nurture?
- Switching to an alternative energy source will provide us with huge benefits.
- Oracy skills should be embedded into every lesson in all subjects.

Motions of value

This is the consideration of whether something is of value or not. To consider this motion, one must first identify a reasonable prerequisite in regard to the relativity of priority.

Examples:

- The concept of free press is a fundamental prerequisite of any democracy.
- Education begins at home, with your home life being one of the biggest influences on your educational achievement.
- A school that has been labelled as 'outstanding' will offer the best education for everyone.

Policy Motions

The proposal of a motion to lobby for the instigation of or change in a policy usually implies the improvement of a current situation through the implementation of actions or requirements.

Examples:

- School uniform/professional attire should be made compulsory for all educational establishments, including colleges and universities.
- Mobile phones must be banned in schools, as they are the source of bullying and distraction.

Of course, organising these topics into clear motions isn't necessarily as clear-cut as it may first appear. To truly exhaust all possible avenues for debate, students must be able to recognise the connectivity of motions and how elements can be adopted in each discussion. The ability to adopt a suitable approach will provide clarity to the subject. At the same time, the recognition of value and relativity will provide definition and scope for the audience. Meanwhile, the policy motions are, in essence, the end result and desired outcome of the debate. The age-old desire to constantly provide solutions to problems exemplifies the need for at least suggestions as to how the issue can be resolved; otherwise the argument is cyclical and lacks rationalisation.

Preparation is key! Promote more developed and well-researched pieces, whether the students do this as individuals or through collaboration.

If your enemy is secure at all points, be prepared for him. If he is in superior strength, evade him. If your opponent is temperamental, seek to irritate him. Pretend to be weak, that he may grow arrogant. If he is taking his ease, give him no rest. If his forces are united, separate them. If sovereign and subject are in accord, put division between them. Attack him where he is unprepared, appear where you are not expected. (Sun Tzu, *The Art of War*)

Preparation is the element of debating that can turn a rant into an argument, where chaos can be brought under control and interpretations can be justified. Preparing for a debate is integral to success, and the skills of preparation and planning can then be transferred into all subjects and all situations where someone is required to provide an extended written or oral response.

To provide outside contextualisation, various jobs now require potential applicants to provide a short presentation on a particular topic. Other applicants, particularly those participating in managerial interviews, are required to complete a written task that gauges their ability to articulate their competence. Preparation and planning are crucial to success. Although we can often be partial to the temptation to 'wing it', more often than not doing so leads us to display less clarity and comprehension, and to come across as being of a lesser calibre than the cool, calm and collected counterpart who has prepared and is ready for whatever may come their way.

In preparing effectively for a debate, there are four key focus points that one should consider:

1. What are the initial interpretations of the statement or topic point?
2. How is the response to be structured?
3. Can you show a recognition of alternatives?
4. Have you considered the rebuttal?

What are the initial interpretations of the statement or topic point?

For this section, students can use the information that they have gathered regarding critical thinking and deeper questioning in order to deploy the most effective strategies of clarification. To start planning and preparing for their address, their first task is to develop a reasonable viewpoint or approach on which to base their ideas and evidence. This element is the 'what', the tip of the iceberg, the 'big idea' or the opening statement on which all of the work will be based. The construction of this standpoint can be strategically centred around four clear consideration points:

- reasoning
- impact
- evidence
- alternatives.

By first recognising and gaining a basic overview of each of these four areas, participants can formulate a reasoned discussion as they develop each point. Whether this is done independently or collaboratively, deeper questioning skills can consequently be adopted to ensure that critical thinking is accessible.

How is the response to be structured?

The structure for a debate is relatively similar to that of a speech. Students can therefore utilise the same skills in both forms of communication, thus supporting their exposure and capacity for mastery.

When students are taught to compose a speech, there are a plethora of structures that can be used in order to scaffold. It would be illogical to provide just one structure and claim that it is the ultimate technique, as in essence that would completely go against the earlier idea that all strategies and techniques are to be considered based on each establishment's context. Providing two different strategies herein will hopefully provide reasonable support that can be adopted and altered where necessary.

The Freytag Pyramid

This technique is aptly named because it can be linked quite nicely to the structural component of plays (or any generalised pieces of fiction). To captivate an audience, the response can easily mimic the graphical tension that is exhibited in a generic five act structure, otherwise referred to as the Freytag Pyramid (Glatch, 2020).

In the nineteenth century, Gustav Freytag, a critic of Greek and Shakespearean drama, came up with a five act dramatic structure to explain effective content. In his interpretation, he specifies:

- The first act contains the exposition. This introduces the characters and setting and ends with an inciting incident.

- The second act complicates the problem created by the inciting incident, frustrating the protagonist's efforts.

- The third act is the climax, in which the fortunes of the protagonist reverse. (In terms of Greek drama, the fortunes of a comic protagonist would go from unlucky to lucky, whilst the fortunes of a tragic protagonist would go from lucky to unlucky.)

- In the fourth act, the results of the protagonist's turn of fortune play out; this may end with a final moment of suspense, such as confrontation between the protagonist and the antagonist that puts the final outcome in doubt.

- Act five, the denouement, documents the consequences of the resolution, and ties up any secondary plots.

In the same way, it could be possible to transfer this understanding into a supportive structure to develop your students' capabilities to present a well-crafted and purposeful speech/debate.

- *Section 1 – The exposition*
    - What is the main focus going to be?
    - What factual statements are you going to present to the audience?
    - Can you entice the audience's interest by setting the scene?
- *Section 2 – The problem/issue*
    - Why have you chosen this stance?
    - What factual and statistical evidence do you have to support your interpretations?
- *Section 3 – The climax*
    - What are the impacts of your proposal?
    - Why is your motion the most logical choice?
    - How will your motion be positive for the audience or society?
- *Section 4 – Recognising the counterargument*
    - What alternative suggestions could be made?
    - What might someone who objects to your motion say?
    - Why is your motion the most rational and obvious choice?
- *Section 5 – Concluding statements*
    - Reiterate your main standpoint.
    - Reinforce your motion and provide a thought-provoking/ emotive closing statement.

Another approach is a more simplistic portrayal of the deeper questioning strategy that was used in the development of questions (the what? how? why? approach). Allowing students to first consider the 'big picture' paves the way for them to develop their ideas in more intrinsic detail.

The 'Big Picture'	*What is our main standpoint on the subject?* *What is the key message that we are attempting to get across to our audience?* *If this were a piece of critical thinking, what would be our thesis statement (the umbrella that links to all of our ideas)?*
A Convincing argument	*What is our 'hook' to gauge the reader's attention?*
Surface level ideas and understanding	*What are examples that we can use to support a piece of writing?* *Can we link our ideas to anything in the news or everyday life to make it relatable?*

Although this is a reduced version of the other two techniques, what this approach allows for is a more condensed strategy that caters for a less prescriptive response. Accessible to all subjects that require extended written responses, a three-tiered approach is one that could easily be adopted in a whole-school strategy.

Can you show a recognition of alternatives?

When developing an effective debate strategy, it is useful to expose students to terms associated with particular standpoints or perspectives. When considering the alternatives available, one must first consider whether the motion is authoritarian or libertarian.

- *Authoritarian*

  - The authoritarian approach is one of strict obedience to rules and regulations that have been introduced and implemented by an autocratic government. Often related to a society run by a dictatorship, all motions are generally detrimental to and enforced at the expense of any personal freedom.

  - When considering your motion, it is advisable to consider whether and to what extent you are petitioning for actual change. Although an authoritarian approach should obviously be discouraged, it should still be recognised that providing a solution to any problems is integral to a logical debate. The ability to provide these solutions can also be deemed a beneficial life skill!

- *Libertarian*

  - A libertarian approach would be one that doesn't advocate for any motions or proposals that would jeopardise the process and concept of free will.

- If students can determine the impact of their approach, they will consequently be able to determine whether or not there may be any detrimental effects that would need to be considered.

- This approach requires the ability to question whether there are any elements of the Human Rights Act that may be infringed through the implementation of a motion or proposal. These can include freedom of speech, expression, movement or trade, etc.

Once this is considered, it is beneficial to explain to students that the key to an effective opening argument is the ability to address questions that will commonly be asked by other students. Responses can then be embedded into the extended speech in order to add more subjectivity to the approach.

✓ Are there issues with the proposal going against the general consensus of the area (does it go against any cultural, political or social values)?

✓ What are the alternative options? Why is this motion the most important one moving forward?

✓ Is this issue one that should be a stand-alone topic, or could it be approached as part of a wider development?

✓ Are there any negative implications or is there any detrimental impact upon its development?

✓ What are the financial stresses that are involved? Where will any necessary money come from and is it financially viable? Is there a long-term cost involved?

✓ Who will be accountable for the development of the motion and its implementation?

Have you considered the rebuttal?

The opportunity to provide a rebuttal is the fundamental characteristic of a speech becoming a debate. Initially allowing students the time and opportunity to prepare and acknowledge questions that could be asked of them during their time on the stand provides students with the encouragement and confidence to partake in communication instead of becoming disengaged or disconnected with the process.

This will not only support confidence, but it will also allow for a wider recognition of a more holistic interpretation of students' own proposed motions and purposes. Although a more active dialogue should be encouraged, when introducing this strategy in the classroom it may be beneficial to provide all students with crib sheets of questions for them to engage with. These rebuttal questions have been recognised for considering alternative perspectives.

- Why is this so important now?
- How does this impact on society?
- Who is affected by the issues?
- Who is affected by the resolution you are suggesting?
- Are there any financial implications (long or short term)?
- Are there any societal impacts that need to be considered?
- Why is this better than the alternative?
- How would a libertarian perceive your motion?
- How would an authoritarian perceive your motion?

If presented to all during the preparation stage, students can prepare their responses without a fear of feeling interrogated. If students can then keep these support sheets or resources, we can begin to form two-way (albeit initially scripted) dialogues. The sheets can also be used to gauge audience listening skills, with the implementation of shorthand note-taking to allow the listeners to consider which questions have been covered thoroughly and which questions it would be best to ask in order to gain greater depth of comprehension.

Consequently, students need to be encouraged to participate in the art of debate throughout their academic career. Being able to participate in a conversation that may elicit a particularly strong emotional response without being perceived negatively is integral to communication in society.

CASE STUDY 11 – ORACY IN HISTORY

Amanda Jacob is a history teacher and an assistant head teacher in a secondary school in Oldham. Her previous roles have been as an advanced skills teacher, head of humanities and head of history.

Developing students' oracy skills in history is crucial. If students can speak like a historian, it often means that they can write like a historian. Speaking like a historian does not happen overnight, and students need to be trained to articulate themselves in an academic way. Within my classroom, there is a focus on their oracy and academic language from their first lesson in year 7. As soon as the students walk through the magic door of the classroom, they develop superpowers and become academic historians. To use these powers properly, they have to use formal language when they contribute to lessons. Students with superpowers model excellence at all times in everything they do. By having these high expectations of oracy from the start, we make students aware that they are not allowed to use slang in their responses or answer questions with simple one-word answers, and that responses with the word 'stuff' is banned in all circumstances.

I use a variety of simple generic techniques to ensure that high standards of oracy are developed within my lessons:

Connectives

In my classroom, there will often be connectives either all around the board or as a wall display. Students are constantly encouraged to refer to these when answering questions in class. Often the students will select one and this will be their connective for the lesson and need to be included in all responses.

To use connectives constantly and develop the oracy of students takes time and practice. It needs patience to be embedded. However, it is crucial to ensure that students can begin to focus and structure their arguments like a historian would do. As a teacher, you need to be firm, polite and patient.

Do not accept the first response from a student if they have either not answered with a full sentence or used a connective at the start. Just smile, be patient and guide them; point to one of the words around the board, reminding them that we model excellence in our oracy as historians. Alternatively, for weaker students, prompt them further after you have asked the question by giving them the word you want their response to begin with and constantly reinforcing this as you work your way around the classroom. Once students understand that you will not accept anything else, it becomes second nature, and they will begin to use this language automatically and even correct or tweak their peer's responses in a positive manner.

Think, pair, share

This is an important technique in developing oracy skills and helping students to talk like historians. An example of this in my classroom would be as follows:

Question: What does the image infer about conditions in an industrial town?

Think:

Students identify different conditions on the image and circle these. They will then share these by talking with their partner.

Student A's initial response with no guidance or structure could be:

'There is a lot of rubbish everywhere and children are playing in it.'

I will model the language that they need to use when sharing their findings and these will also be written on the board to remind them to remain focussed and use the language from the question, being focussed as a historian.

Pair:

Student A goes first and beings with: 'Firstly, I can see... This infers **that** conditions were... **because...**'

Student B will then respond with: 'In addition, I can see... this infers **that** conditions were ... **because...**'

Before we move to whole-class feedback, I will ask them to level up their language as historians and tweak some of the words they use. I put up common words that they may have initially included in their responses and then ask them to replace these with words a historian would use, and write these in the blank table.

Level up these words in your response	Synonyms a historian would use
Bad	Negative
Dirty	Unhygienic
Lots of people	Overcrowded
Smelly	pungent

Share:

We will then move on to whole-class feedback. At this point there will just be the image on the board and the sentence prompts will have been removed. Students can come up to the board, identify and circle their feature, and then tell the rest of the class what it infers and why. They are encouraged to write what it infers using their levelled-up language in a few words around the image. When feeding back, language is constantly levelled up.

Student A: 'Firstly, I can see that industrial towns were overcrowded and unhygienic, as there are a lot of people living there and the children are playing in the rubbish. This infers living conditions were poor and that disease would easily spread, as there was a lack of cleanliness.'

I try to **avoid abbreviations** and, if feeling very brave, there will be the slang police in the classroom (normally a lively student who finds it, on occasion, challenging to focus). Their crucial role is to point out each time, in a non-threatening manner (e.g. raising their hand and not shouting out), when incorrect language, slang, or an abbreviation has been used. I or the student then need to reword and repeat their sentence in a more formal manner as a historian would do. This is a really fun, simple activity to implement in a classroom, and raises oracy standards instantly.

CONCLUSION

Initially, I structured this conclusion to provide a summary of advice that appeared more structured for each specific role that you might find in an educational establishment. However, this would have compartmentalised and segregated an approach that needs to be embodied and understood in its entirety.

We all need to read the signs and communicate effectively. We all need to recognise any barriers or potential indicators. We all need to encourage the implementation of oracy skills to support our learners with one of the most valuable life skills that we could bestow on them before they enter the next stage in their lives.

If these cultures and approaches are not already embedded, this is by no means an easy feat. There may be times that you long for silence. Times where you feel dishevelled and like your voice is being engulfed in a sea of chatter. It is at times like this that it is important to recognise that the fundamental approaches that we may (as practitioners) take for granted take time and explicit reference to master. Your learners may not leave your classroom spouting thesis statements and talking eloquently with their friends. They may remain provincial in their speech. This isn't a bad thing. If, through the incorporation of oracy into your curriculum, students are able to articulate their thoughts with confidence and without fear, then you're on the right steps to success!

Some top tips to help you get started:

- **Don't be afraid to start small.**

Often when decisions are made immediately, without consultation or further development, there can be a stigma attached, even if the approach will provide substantial improvement. You have to consider your audience and your objectives. You can then assess the most logical approach to ensure consistency and adoption from all stakeholders.

- **Create research groups to encourage ownership and collaboration.**

Both staff and students can further their skills by collaborating with others. For students, this could be the assessing of clubs and societies that could be established to support oracy in the curriculum (debate club or philosophy circles). For staff, this could be teaching and learning research and developing strategies and suggestions to support others.

- **Listen to any feedback provided and act where required to ensure clarity of purpose and approach.**

It is easy when you have invested time and energy into a strategy to stick with this approach to embed it into everyday practice. However, to support this, it is important to encourage a cyclical structure model that will promote constant reflection and improvement.

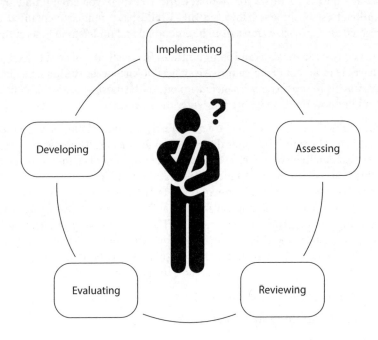

- **Manage the consistency.** Success derives from a team effort, not the blood, sweat and tears of one individual. To support the development of oracy, you may need to change the culture. Whether this is encouraging students to have a voice or encouraging peers to adopt more dialogic strategies, no approaches can ever be embedded without the support of colleagues and peers. It's important that all stakeholders are on the same page and are encouraging these techniques in their general practice. This will help students to be more pliable in the implementation of new strategies.

- **Model high expectations.**

Unfortunately, we sometimes exhibit a tendency towards misconceptions of boundaries and limitations in learning. By becoming engrossed in the presentation of techniques that may demonstrate a hierarchy of learning capabilities, we have supported a glass ceiling under which the students risk becoming trapped. Remember that all students can achieve higher-order thinking; it is just the HOW that may differ.

- **Don't be afraid of the noise.**

Often approaches are altered or redacted too quickly. This can usually arise because of issues with behaviour and/or a lack of immediate progress. We need to understand that short-term approaches lead to short-term outcomes. Try to allow learners the time to embed expectations before hitting any proverbial panic button.

- **Barriers can often be see-through.**

Communication barriers don't necessarily imply a lack of comprehension. Often, frustration comes from a failure to recognise the extent of understanding. We can easily respond to the claustrophobic feeling of a lack of ability to interact by over-simplifying tasks or non-verbal communication, which can come across as condescending. We all have that one relative who turns communicating into a loud game of charades whenever they travel to a non-English-speaking country!

- **Make every voice count.**

Frustration and misunderstanding are often the two biggest catalysts to a breakdown in communication. Although there will be moments where these situations appear inevitable, there are still cues and signs (both verbal and non-verbal) that can help us diffuse and possibly even prevent a situation from occurring if we recognise them.

- **Make conversations count!**

Remember that communication isn't a one-sided skill. Effective dialogue derives from listeners and reflectors just as much as those who are making the noise!

It's time to put oracy back into the triad so that we can prepare our students in a skill that they will need throughout their lives.

It's only through talking about oracy that we can truly begin to communicate with one another whilst supporting the communication of others!

REFERENCES

Accent Bias Britain (2019). [Website] Retrieved from: https://accentbiasbritain. org/, [accessed 12/09/20].

Alexander, R.J. (2005). Talk for Learning the Second Year, *Evaluation of North Yorkshire County Council Talk for Learning Project 2004.*

Alexander, R. (2018). Developing dialogic teaching: genesis, process, trial, *Research Papers in Education.*

Alexander, R. (2019). Dialogic Teaching, Robin Alexander [website], March 2019. Retrieved from https://robinalexander.org.uk/dialogic-teaching/, [accessed 10/09/2020].

AQA (2015). *Spoken Language Endorsement for GCSE English Language* [report]. https://filestore.aqa.org.uk/resources/english/AQA-8700-SL-ENDORSEMENT. PDF, [accessed 25/10/2020].

Beck, I.L., McKeown, M.G. and Kucan, L. (2013). *Bringing words to life: robust vocabulary instruction.* New York, NY: Guilford.

Bell Foundation, the (2018). EAL [website]. Retrieved from: https://www. bell-foundation.org.uk/app/uploads/2018/11/Language-for-Results-Call-for-Partners.pdf, [accessed 08/09/2020].

Bercow, J. (2008). Bercow Review of Services for children and young people with speech, language and communication needs [article]. Retrieved from: https:// dera.ioe.ac.uk/8405/7/7771-dcsf-bercow_Redacted.pdf, [accessed 06/09/20].

Brännström K.J., Holm L, Lyberg-Åhlander, V., Haake, M., Kastberg, T. and Sahlén, B. (2015). Children's subjective ratings and opinions of typical and dysphonic voice after performing a language comprehension task in background noise, *J Voice*, Volume 29, Issue 5, pp. 624–630.

Britton, J.N. (1993). *Language and Learning*, 2nd edn. Portsmouth, NH: Boynton/Cook Publishers.

Bromley, M. (2017). Teaching Practise: Dialogic Questioning, *SecEd* [article]. Retrieved from: https://www.sec-ed.co.uk/best-practice/teaching-practice-dialogic-questioning/, [accessed 10/09/2020].

Brooks, R. (2016). How to offend and confuse people around the world without saying a word [blog], 17/06/2016. Retrieved from: https://k-international.com/blog/nonverbal-communication-across-cultures/, [accessed 07/09/20].

Cherry, K. (2020). The 4 stages of cognitive development: background and key concepts of Piaget's theory, Verywell Mind [website], 21/03/2020. Retrieved from: https://www.verywellmind.com/piagets-stages-of-cognitive-development-2795457, [accessed 04/09/2020].

Clark, D. (2020). English as an additional language in schools in England 2018, *Statista* [website], 11/06/2020. Retrieved from: https://www.statista.com/statistics/331675/england-region-english-additional-language-primary-pupils/, [accessed 07/09/20].

Dawes, L. (2018). Teaching Tone of voice [article], Oracy Cambridge, 19/09/2018. Retrieved from https://oracycambridge.org/2018/09/19/teaching-tone-of-voice/, [accessed 12/09/20].

Department for Education (2014). *The National Curriculum in England: Key Stages 1 and 2 framework.*

The Department for Education (2014). *The National Curriculum in England: Key Stages 3 and 4 framework.*

Department for Education (2016). *EAL Levels of Competence and the DfE proficiency scale,* Solihull Metropolitan borough [website]. Retrieved from https://socialsolihull.org.uk/schools/sab/wp-content/uploads/2016/07/EAL-Learner-Overview-Docx-with-DFE-Descriptors.pdf, [accessed 07/09/2020].

Department for Education (2018). *Key stage 2 and multi-academy trust performance 2018* (revised).

Department for Education (2018). *Key Stage 4 including multi-academy trust performance 2018* (revised) [publication], 24/01/2018. Retrieved from https://assets.publishing.service.gov.uk/government/uploads/system/uploads/attachment_data/file/774014/2018_KS4_main_text.pdf, [accessed 07/09/2020].

Dockrell, J., Lindsay, G., Law, J., and Roulstone, S. (2015). Supporting children with speech, language and communication needs: an overview of the results of the Better Communication Research Programme, *International Journal of Language and Communication Disorders*, Volume 49, Issue 5, pp. 543–557.

Dockrell, J., Ricketts, J. and Lindsay, G. (2012). *Understanding speech, language and communication needs: Profiles of need and provision.* London: Department for Education research report. [Report] 27/12/2012. Retrieved from https://www.gov.uk/government/collections/better-communication-research-programme, [accessed 21/09/2020].

Dweck, C. (2006). *Mindset: The new psychology of success.* London: Random House.

Education Endowment Foundation (EEF) (2018). Retrieved from: https://educationendowmentfoundation.org.uk/pdf/generate/?u=https://educationendowmentfoundation.org.uk/pdf/toolkit/?id=150&t=Teaching%20and%20Learning%20Toolkit&e=150&s=, [accessed 21/09/2020].

Edwards, C.H. (1981). A second look at direct instruction, *High School Journal,* Volume 64, Issue 4, pp.166–169.

Ekman, P. (1972). Universals and Cultural Differences in Facial Expressions of Emotions. In Cole, J. (ed.) *Nebraska Symposium on Motivation,* (pp. 207–282). Lincoln, NE: University of Nebraska Press.

English-Speaking Union (2020). What is oracy? [website]. Retrieved from https://www.esu.org/oracy/ [accessed 21/09/2020].

Gaunt, A. and Stott, A. (2019). *Transform teaching and learning through talk: the oracy imperative.* London: Rowman & Littlefield.

Glatch, S. (2020). The 5 Elements of Dramatic Structure: Understanding Freytag's Pyramid, Writers.com [article], 12/05/2020. Retrieved from: https://writers.com/freytags-pyramid, [accessed 25/10/2020].

Gleeson, B. (2016). 5 Tips for improving leadership communication, *Forbes* [article], 23/05/2016. Retrieved from https://www.forbes.com/sites/brentgleeson/2016/05/23/5-tips-for-improving-leadership-communication/#60b4bea54b7d, [accessed 12/09/2020].

Gonzales, N., Moll, L.C. and Amanti, C. (eds) (2006). *Funds of knowledge: theorizing practices in households, communities and classrooms.* Abingdon: Routledge.

Hall, E.T. (1966). *The Hidden Dimension: An anthropologist examines man's use of space in public and in private.* Garden City, NY: Doubleday.

International Baccalaureate (2020). Facts and figures [website]. Retrieved from: https://ibo.org/about-the-ib/facts-and-figures/, [accessed 07/09/20].

Jay T., Willis, B. and Thomas, P. et al. (2017). *Dialogic Teaching: Evaluation report and executive summary.* Education Endowment Foundation.

Joint Council for Qualifications (2020). *Adjustments for candidates with disabilities and learning difficulties* [publication]. Retrieved from file:///C:/Users/Account/Downloads/AA-regs-2020-2021-version-for-website.pdf, [accessed 07/09/20].

Kirschner, P.A., Sweller, J. and Clark, R.E. (2006). Why Minimal Guidance During Instruction Does Not Work: An analysis of the failure of constructivist, discovery, problem-based, experiential, and inquiry-based teaching, *Educational Psychologist,* Volume 41, Issue 2, pp. 75–86.

Klein, N. (2018). You make decisions quicker and based on less information than you think, *The Conversation* [blog], 10/12/2018. Retrieved from https://theconversation.com/you-make-decisions-quicker-and-based-on-less-information-than-you-think-108460, [accessed 12/09/2020].

Lee, W. (2013). *Talk of the Town evaluation report* [report]. The Communication Trust. Retrieved from: http://www.thecommunicationtrust.org.uk/media/32943/talk_of_the_town_evaluation_report.pdf, [accessed 21/09/2020].

Lemov, D., Driggs, C. and Woolway, E. (2016). *Reading reconsidered: a practical guide to rigorous literacy instruction.* San Francisco, CA: Jossey Bass.

Martins, R.H., Pereira, E.R., Hidalgo, C.B. and Tavares, E.L. (2014). Voice disorders in teachers. A review, *J Voice,* Volume 28, pp. 716–724.

McGill, R. (2019). *UCL Verbal Feedback Project* [report], August 2019. Retrieved from https://www.ucl.ac.uk/widening-participation/sites/widening-participation/files/2019_verbal_feedback_project_final_4_print.pdf, [accessed 12/09/20].

Mehrabian, A. (1972). *Nonverbal Communication.* London: Transaction Publishers.

Mercer, N. and Littleton, K. (2007). *Dialogue and the development of children's thinking: a sociocultural approach.* London: Routledge.

Mercer, N. and Hodgkinson, S. (eds) (2008). *Exploring Talk in School: Inspired by the work of Douglas Barnes.* London: Sage.

Ministry of Housing, Communities & Local Government (2019). *English indices of deprivation 2019: mapping resources* [report], 26/09/2019. Retrieved from: https://www.gov.uk/government/statistics/english-indices-of-deprivation-2019, [accessed 21/09/20].

Moon, J. (1999). Reflection in Learning and Professional Development [resource]. Retrieved from https://dera.ioe.ac.uk/12995/1/4215.pdf, [accessed 25/10/2020].

National Literacy Trust (2018). *Literacy and life expectancy* [research], 15/02/2018. Retrieved from: https://literacytrust.org.uk/research-services/research-reports/literacy-and-life-expectancy/, [accessed 21/09/20].

National Literacy Trust (2019). Language unlocks reading: supporting early language and reading for every child [article]. Retrieved from: https://literacytrust.org.uk/policy-and-campaigns/all-party-parliamentary-group-literacy/language-unlocks-reading/, [accessed 21/09/20].

Nesari, A.J. (2015). 6th World Conference on Psychology, *Counseling and Guidance Procedia – Social and Behavioural Sciences*, Volume 205, pp. 642–647.

OFSTED, (2019). *Education Inspection Framework*, [report]. Retrieved from: https://www.gov.uk/government/collections/education-inspection-framework, [accessed 25/10/20].

Pearson (2016). England: What makes an effective teacher (Series 9 of 23), pp. 1–17.

Postholm, M.B. (2013). Classroom Management: what does research tell us?, *European Educational Research Journal*, Volume 12, Issue 3.

Priestley, J. (2009). *An Inspector Calls*. Stuttgart: Klett Sprachen.

Quigley, A. (2018). *Closing the vocabulary gap*. Abingdon: Routledge.

Quigley, A., Muijs, D. and Stringer, E. (2018). *Metacognition and self-regulated learning: guidance report*. Education Endowment Foundation.

Resnick, L.B., Michaels, S. and O'Connor, M.C. (2010). How (well-structured) talk builds the mind. In Preiss, D.D. & Sternberg, R.J. (eds) *Innovations in educational psychology: Perspectives on learning, teaching, and human development*, (p. 163–194). New York, NY: Springer Publishing Company.

Rodrigues, A., Medeiros, A. and Teixeira, L. (2017). Impact of the teacher's voice in the classroom: a literature review. *Revistas* [article]. Retrieved from https://revistas.pucsp.br/index.php/dic/article/viewFile/29063/22851, [accessed 08/09/20].

Schuelka, M.J. (2018). Implementing inclusive education, knowledge, evidence and learning for development [website], 29/08/2018. Retrieved from: https://assets.publishing.service.gov.uk/media/5c6eb77340f0b647b214c599/374_Implementing_Inclusive_Education.pdf, [accessed 06/09/2020].

Shakespeare, W. (2006). *As You Like It*, 3rd rev edn. London: The Arden Shakespeare.

Sherrington, T. (2017). *The Learning Rainforest*. Woodbridge: John Catt Educational Ltd.

Sherrington, T. and Stafford, S. (2019). Dialogic Questioning. Questioning Techniques. Chartered College of Teaching.

Stevie, D. (2020). 5 Non-verbal teaching techniques of successful foreign language educators, *FluentU: General Educator Blog* [blog]. Retrieved from: https://www.fluentu.com/blog/educator/language-teaching-techniques/#:~:text=Body%20Language%3A%205%20Powerful%20Non-verbal%20Teaching%20Techniques%20That,Voice%20Modulation.%20...%205%20Positive%20Force%20Field.%20, [accessed 08/09/20].

Sutton Trust and Carnegie Corporation of New York (2012). *The Social Mobility Summit* [report], May 2012. Retrieved from https://www.suttontrust.com/wp-content/uploads/2020/01/social-mobility-summit2012.pdf, [accessed 21/09/20].

Tanenbaum (2016). Combating Extremism [resource], 7/12/2016. Retrieved from: https://tanenbaum.org/wp-content/uploads/2016/12/7-Principles-for-Inclusive-Education-Summary.pdf, [accessed 06/09/2020].

Tennent, W., Reedy, D., Hobsbaum, A. and Gamble, N. (2016). *Guiding readers – layers of meaning: a handbook for teaching reading comprehension to 7–11 year olds*. London: UCL Press.

The Communication Code (2014). Communicating the Code [website]. Retrieved from: https://www.thecommunicationtrust.org.uk/media/362413/ctc_all_sections_with_links.pdf, [accessed 07/09/20].

Thiran, R. Why, How, What? (2010). *Leaderonomics.com* [article]. Retrieved from https://leaderonomics.com/business/why-how-what, [accessed 12/09/2020].

Thompson, S. (2020). Creating a challenging and coherent curriculum for progress and pleasure. In Sealey, C. and Bennett, T. (eds), *The curriculum: an evidence-informed guide for teachers*, (pp. 49–58). Woodbridge: John Catt Educational Ltd.

UKEssays (2018). Theories of Communication and Language Acquisition [online]. Retrieved from: https://www.ukessays.com/essays/childcare/theories-communication-language-3571.php?vref=1, [accessed 04/09/2020].

UNESCO (2017). UNESCO. Assistant Director-General for Education, 2010–2018 (Qian Tang). writer of foreword [1763].

Voice 21 (2019). *The Oracy Benchmarks.* [publication]. Retrieved from:https://voice21.org/wp-content/uploads/2020/06/Benchmarks-report-FINAL.pdf, [accessed 04/08/2020].

Wang, J. (2009). 7 Non-verbal Cues and What They (Probably) Mean, *Entrepreneur*, May, p. 15.

Willingham, D.T. (2009). *Why don't students like school?* San Francisco, CA: Jossey Bass.

Zandan, N. (2020) Eye Contact – A Declining communications tool?, *Quantified Communications* [blog]. Retrieved from: https://www.quantifiedcommunications.com/blog/eye-contact-a-declining-communications-tool/#:~:text=However%2C%20to%20make%20an%20emotional%20connection%2C%20the%20ideal,unnerving%20for%20the%-20person%20you%20are%20talking%20to, [accessed 08/09/20].

Epigraph sources

Why focus on oracy?*Make thyself a craftsman in speech, for thereby thou shalt gain the upper hand.* Zimmer, J. (2014). Quotes for Public Speakers, *Manner of Speaking*, [blog] 16.04.1994. Retrieved from: https://mannerofspeaking.org/2014/04/16/quotes-for-public-speakers-no-178-ancient-egypt/, [accessed 25/10/2020].

Understanding the key to effective communication. *When people talk, listen completely. Most people never listen.* (Hemingway). BrainyQuote.com. Ernest Hemingway Quotes. BrainyQuote.Com, 2020 [website]. Retrieved from: https://www.brainyquote.com/quotes/ernest_hemingway_383060, [accessed 25/10/20].

Understanding the key to effective communication. *Nature has given us two ears, two eyes, and but one tongue – to the end that we should hear and see more than we speak.* (Socrates). Juma, N. (2020). 80 Socrates Quotes On Life, Wisdom & Philosophy To Inspire You, Everyday Power, [article] 26/02/2020. Retrieved from: https://everydaypower.com/socrates-quotes/, [accessed 25/10/2020].

How oracy skills support classroom management. *A wonderful fact to reflect upon, that every human creature is constituted to be that profound secret and mystery to every other.* (Charles Dickens). *A Tale of Two Cities*, CliffsNotes [website]. Retrieved from: https://www.cliffsnotes.com/literature/t/a-tale-of-two-cities/summary-and-analysis/book-1-chapter-3/book-1-chapter-3-1, [accessed 25/10/2020].

Changing the dialogue. *Every art and every inquiry, and similarly every action and choice, is thought to aim at some good; and for this reason the good has rightly been declared to be that at which all things aim.* (Aristotle). Archie, L. and Archie, J.G. The Reading Selection from the Nicomachean Ethics. A Brief Introduction to Philosophical Thinking [article]. Retrieved from: https://philosophy.lander.edu/intro/introbook2.1/x5935.html, [accessed 25/10/20].

Monologic or dialogic approaches to learning. *I never teach my pupils, I only attempt to provide the conditions in which they can learn.* (Einstein). GoodReads, Albert Einstein, Quotes. Retrieved from: https://www.goodreads. com/quotes/253933-i-never-teach-my-pupils-i-only-attempt-to-provide, [accessed 25/10/20].

Monologic or dialogic approaches to learning. *The task of the modern educator is not to cut down jungles, but to irrigate deserts.* (C.S. Lewis). Dickieson, B. (2012). Irrigating Deserts: C.S. Lewis on Education by Joel D. Heck, *A Pilgrim in Narnia* [blog] 22/05/2012. Retrieved from: https://apilgriminnarnia. com/2012/05/22/irrigating-deserts/, [accessed 25/10/2020].

Monologic or dialogic approaches to learning. *A leader is best when people barely know he exists, when his work is done, his aim fulfilled, they will say: we did it ourselves.* (Lao Tzu). BrainyQuote.com, Lao Tzu Quotes. BrainyQuote. Com, 2020 [website]. Retrieved from: https://www.brainyquote.com/quotes/ lao_tzu_121709, [accessed 25/10/20].

Finding your balance through oracy. *Questioning is the only defensible form of teaching.* (Socrates). Juma, N. (2020). 80 Socrates Quotes On Life, Wisdom & Philosophy To Inspire You, Everyday Power, [article] 26/02/2020. Retrieved from: https://everydaypower.com/socrates-quotes/, [accessed 25/10/2020].

Potential breakdowns in communication. *10% of conflict is due to difference in opinion. 90% is due to wrong tone of voice.* (Ritu Ghatourey). Marks, E. (2015). 10% of conflict is due to difference of opinion and 90% is due to delivery and tone of voice, *LinkedIn* [blog] 09/09/2015. Retrieved from: https://www. linkedin.com/pulse/10-conflict-due-difference-opinion-90-delivery-tone-voice-eve-marks, [accessed 25/10/2020].

The art of debate. *Don't raise your voice, improve your argument.* Desmond Tutu [Address at the Nelson Mandela Foundation in Houghton, Johannesburg, South Africa, 23 November 2004]. GoodReads, Desmond Tutu, Quotes. Retrieved from: https://www.goodreads.com/quotes/213415-don-t-raise-your-voice-improve-your-argument-address-at-the, [accessed 25/10/20].

The art of debate. *By the very act of arguing, you awake the patient's reason; and once it is awake, who can foresee the result?* (C.S. Lewis). Lewis, C.S. (2014). *The Screwtape Letters*, Freeditorial Publishing house [synopsis], 14/04/2014. Retrieved from: https://freeditorial.com/en/books/the-screwtape-letters, [accessed 25/10/2020].

The art of debate. *If your enemy is secure at all points, be prepared for him. If he is in superior strength, evade him. If your opponent is temperamental, seek to irritate him. Pretend to be weak, that he may grow arrogant. If he is taking his ease, give him no rest. If his forces are united, separate them. If sovereign and subject are in accord, put division between them. Attack him where he is unprepared, appear where you are not expected.* (Sun Tzu). Jackson, E. Sun Tzu's 31 Best Pieces of Leadership, 'State of the Nation' [article], 27/11/2017. Retrieved from: https://stateofthenation2012.com/?p=89914, [accessed 25/10/2020].